KJV DEVOTIONAL

in the
Morning
and
in the
Evening

NICK HARRISON

HARVEST HOUSE PUBLISHERS
EUGENE, OREGON

All Scripture quotations are taken from the King James Version of the Bible.

Cover photo © Dugan Design Group / Unsplash
Cover design by Dugan Design Group
Interior design by KUHN Design Group

For bulk, special sales, or ministry purchases, please call 1-800-547-8979.
Email: Customerservice@hhpbooks.com

M This logo is a federally registered trademark of the Hawkins Children's LLC.
Harvest House Publishers, Inc., is the exclusive licensee of this trademark.

KJV Devotional in the Morning and in the Evening
Copyright © 2023 by Harvest House Publishers
Published by Harvest House Publishers
Eugene, Oregon 97408
www.harvesthousepublishers.com

ISBN 978-0-7369-8787-5 (hardcover)
ISBN 978-0-7369-8788-2 (eBook)

Library of Congress Control Number: 2023934552

Printed in Colombia

23 24 25 26 27 28 29 30 31 / NI / 10 9 8 7 6 5 4 3 2 1

I f you're a lover of the King James Version (KJV) of the Bible, you're far from alone. Even with the plethora of new translations of Scripture, the KJV still ranks high among the bestselling Bible translations.

And it's no wonder. Down through generation after generation of Christians, the KJV has been loved, quoted, memorized, and praised. Even unbelievers are fans. Writers such as skeptic and Nobel Prize winner George Bernard Shaw and Pulitzer Prize winner Eudora Welty have sung its praises. The great British statesman Winston Churchill said of the KJV, "The scholars who produced this masterpiece are mostly unknown and unremembered. But they forged an enduring link, literary and religious, between the English-speaking people of the world."

The "Authorized" King James Version of the Bible was the result of King James I of England's direction that a translation of the Bible be readied for the Church of England. Seven years later in 1611, after the painstaking work of forty-seven qualified men, the new Bible was published—not as the King James Version or Authorized version (that designation would come two centuries later) but as the more cumbersome *The Holy Bible, Conteyning the Old Testament, and the New: Newly Translated out of the Originall Tongues: & with the Former Translations Diligently Compared and Revised by His Majesties Speciall Comandement.*

It should be noted that all the translators were well aware of the gravity of their task. All were university graduates—many from Oxford and Cambridge. With precision, they diligently crafted the monumental book that has served generation after generation of Christian believers.

Because the KJV has been so loved by so many in previous generations, it occurred to me to conclude each devotion on the following pages with a relevant quote from some of the godly men and women of the past, no doubt many of whom used the KJV exclusively. For that reason, I've selected a handful of some of the best preachers and writers of the past. A few names you'll likely immediately recognize— Charles Spurgeon, Oswald Chambers, A.W. Tozer, Elisabeth Elliot— while others will be new to you. For instance, though many know of Spurgeon through his thirty-eight years as pastor of London's Metropolitan Tabernacle, few have heard of James Smith, his predecessor at what was then called New Park Street Chapel. At the time, his writings were even more popular than Spurgeon's. Other names I hope you'll want to become acquainted with include J.C. Ryle, Octavius Winslow, Amy Carmichael, J.C. Philpot, Thomas Watson, and many others whose long-ago writings still minister to Christians today. For instance, Hannah Whitall Smith wrote one of the best-selling Christian books of all time, *The Christian's Secret of a Happy Life.* First published in 1875, it's still in print and widely read today.

Just as it's important to keep the KJV close at hand, we would do well to also revisit the writings of these oft-neglected men and women of the faith. Though these valiant warriors have passed on, their message echoes down through the years.

Now, may God bless you as you grow closer to Him, day by day, evening by evening.

> *The LORD will command his lovingkindness in the day time, and in the night his song shall be with me, and my prayer unto the God of my life.*
>
> PSALM 42:8

A BRAND-NEW DAY

This is the day which the LORD hath made;
we will rejoice and be glad in it.
PSALM 118:24

Rejoicing in a new day, fresh from the hand of God, is a decision we must make. Often, it's not a decision we want to make. We might prefer to roll over for another forty winks, take a drive to the beach, watch a movie—anything that would keep us from certain responsibilities.

But we do rise from our bed, we dress, and we prepare for another day. In preparing ourselves for the day, however, we must also make that decision to rejoice. We must not rely on feelings nor embrace anxiety about what the day may bring—we must only rejoice in the Lord.

God made this day. He made it for us. Whatever it holds has passed through His hands already. Rejoicing is our way of meeting the day—every new day—head-on.

So set aside your worries. Rejoice and be glad in this new day fashioned by God for you.

"When you cannot rejoice in feelings, circumstances
or conditions, rejoice in the Lord."
A.B. SIMPSON

HE WILL HEAR MY VOICE

*Evening, and morning, and at noon, will I pray,
and cry aloud: and he shall hear my voice.*

PSALM 55:17

Today was a gift from God. Now it draws to a close. What is done is done. Tomorrow awaits. But tonight, as you end the day in prayer, feel free to find a place to be alone and pray out loud. Not *loud*, but out loud. There is something about voicing our prayers that stimulates faith. Yes, God hears our silent prayers, but for generations before us, Christian men and women have often given voice to their prayers.

Tonight, thank God for another day, and relax in the knowledge that He has prepared a new tomorrow for you to use in His service. No matter how you pray—silently or aloud—know that God hears. And just as the day began with a choice to rejoice, may it also end with rejoicing.

> *"The physical voice we use in prayer need not be
> great nor startling; even should we not lift up any
> great cry or shout, God will yet hear us."*
>
> ORIGEN

THE VERY FIRST THING

Seek ye first the kingdom of God, and his righteousness;
and all these things shall be added unto you.

MATTHEW 6:33

We are a generation of seekers. We want this and we want that. But Jesus cautions us about the most important "want" of all—the kingdom of God.

Today is God's new day for you. And you will no doubt have things you must seek at work, at home, or in some important activity. But throughout the day, each of us must have the certainty that among all our duties—and amid all our seeking—God's kingdom and His righteousness must be first. All else that is necessary for us will be added.

"If thou needest health, seek it; but seek first the kingdom
of God. If thou desirest knowledge, seek it; but seek first
that fear of the Lord which is the beginning of wisdom. If
thou wantest wealth, seek it in that moderate way which
is allowable to thee; but first of all let thy treasure be in
heaven. Seek thy God first, before everything else."

CHARLES SPURGEON

THE VERY LAST THING

*All thy works shall praise thee, O Lord; and thy saints
shall bless thee. They shall speak of the glory of thy kingdom,
and talk of thy power; to make known to the sons of men his
mighty acts, and the glorious majesty of his kingdom.*

PSALM 145:10-12

Seeking God's kingdom has been our daily quest. Now, as the evening has come, we retire with the kingdom of God still on our mind. This earthly kingdom will pass away. But we shall one day set foot in that new kingdom where we will never grow old, nor have the need for evening rest. This kingdom is filled with glorious majesty—and it's all for us!

Tonight, set aside any troubling situations that are tied to this present earthly kingdom. What is here now will eventually pass. Even at day's end, make God's kingdom the very last thing on your mind. You will then rest well.

*"I place no value on anything I have or may possess,
except in relation to the kingdom of God."*

DAVID LIVINGSTONE

THE GOD WHO IS SOVEREIGN

I will say of the LORD, He is my refuge and my fortress:
my God; in him will I trust.

PSALM 91:2

Is God sovereign? Does He control the destinies of us all? If He is not sovereign, if He is in some way handicapped from intervening on our behalf, then why do we bother to pray?

But of course God *is* sovereign. He has covenanted with us to hear and answer our prayers. Only a sovereign God can make and keep such a promise. We need have no fear of over-trusting God. He is our refuge. Our fortress. In Him we can confidently trust. Even dark clouds cannot diminish His sovereignty. Instead, He can turn those clouds inside out to reveal their silver lining.

"To the one who delights in the sovereignty of God the
clouds not only have a 'silver lining' but they are silvern all
through, the darkness only serving to offset the light!"

A.W. PINK

GOD'S SOVEREIGN HAND

Thou shalt not be afraid for the terror by night.

PSALM 91:5

God has exercised His sovereignty on your behalf today whether it was apparent or not. Daily, He orchestrates events for your ultimate good. You trusted His sovereignty today, and you can trust it tonight. God is at work even as you wind down from the day, and later, as you sleep. You need not be fearful of anything—His hand is still upon you as you lay in your bed. Sleep well tonight in the full presence of your Creator. Trust even your sleep to the sovereign hand of God.

"Remember that Almighty God is about your bed, and sees your down-lying, and your uprising; understands your thoughts, and is acquainted with all your ways. Remember likewise that his holy angels, who [guard and watch] over you all night, does also behold how you wake and rise. Do all things, therefore, as in the solemn presence of God, and in the sight of his holy angels."

LEWIS BAYLY

MORNING JOY

We glory in tribulations also: knowing that
tribulation worketh patience; and patience,
experience; and experience, hope.

ROMANS 5:3-4

When we encounter trials and tribulations, we mostly think about how soon we can get through them and enjoy peace once again. The apostle Paul had a different attitude. He *gloried* in his many tribulations! Why did he do that? Because he saw the purpose behind life's challenges: to bring about patience. Every trial received with the expectancy of building patience and hope through experience should be welcomed by all who wish to grow spiritually.

It's right to pray our way through our trials—that, too, builds our faith. But patience, the fruit of trials, is what we wish to harvest.

"Your head may be crowned with thorny troubles now but it
shall wear a sparkling crown before long. Your hand may be
filled with cares but it shall sweep the strings of the harp of
Heaven soon. Your garments may be soiled with dust now but
they shall be snow-white by-and-by. Wait a little longer."

CHARLES SPURGEON

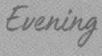
EVENING JOY

Day unto day uttereth speech,
and night unto night showeth knowledge.

PSALM 19:2

Our daytime trials work patience in us, but in the evening we take time to refresh, setting aside any remaining daytime challenges. Now we take time to look up and see the starry sky and wonder at God's greatness. Our Father did all that!

During the day those stars are still there. We just can't see them because of the sun's light. But night after night we see God in the vastness of the universe. The day may uttereth speech, but night after night shows forth the knowledge of God.

> *"Each successive night [shows forth knowledge respecting*
> *God]. It is done by the stars in their courses; in their order;*
> *their numbers; their ranks; their changes of position; their*
> *rising and their setting. There are as many lessons conveyed*
> *to man about the greatness and majesty of God by the silent*
> *movements of each night as there are by the light of the successive*
> *days just as there may be as many lessons conveyed to the soul*
> *about God in the dark night of affliction and adversity, as*
> *there are when the sun of prosperity shines upon us."*

ALBERT BARNES

BURDENS RELEASED

Come unto me, all ye that labor and are heavy laden,
and I will give you rest.

MATTHEW 11:28

It seems ironic to begin the day with a call to rest. Isn't daytime our working, errand-running, household duties time? Yes, but to be most effective in all we do, we must begin the day by hearing our Lord say, "Come unto me" and then take Him at His word when He promises rest for the day.

Not only are our duties made lighter, but our daily burdens are released as we rest in Christ. He who knows what our day holds is acquainted with our responsibilities, and sees our burdens will supply the strength to do all that's required of us…if we first rest in Him.

"We can easily manage if we will only take, each day, the
burden appointed to it. But the load will be too heavy for us
if we carry yesterday's burden over again today, and then add
the burden of the morrow before we are required to bear it."

JOHN NEWTON

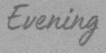
BURDENS LIFTED

My yoke is easy, and my burden is light.
MATTHEW 11:30

How was it for you today? Were your burdens released? Was God present as you went about your day? And what about tonight? Is the burden still with the Lord, or has it eased its way back onto your shoulders?

What was placed in God's able hands today must stay there tonight. When God receives a burden, He will not return it to us for another round of anxiety. Time now to remember that all your burdens, light or heavy, are no longer yours to bear.

Rest easy tonight. The God who heard your prayer today has remembered it this evening.

> *"What is needed for happy effectual service is simply to put your work into the Lord's hand, and leave it there. Do not take it to Him in prayer, saying, 'Lord, guide me, Lord, give me wisdom, Lord, arrange for me,' and then arise from your knees, and take the burden all back, and try to guide and arrange for yourself. Leave it with the Lord, and remember that what you trust to Him you must not worry over nor feel anxious about. Trust and worry cannot go together."*
> HANNAH WHITALL SMITH

ALWAYS TRIUMPHANT!

Thanks be unto God, which always
causeth us to triumph in Christ.

2 CORINTHIANS 2:14

Every life fully given to Christ will face trials, temptations, and often persecution. But God enables every trusting believer to triumph over them all. There is no situation for which God does not have an answer. We need not triumph over trouble in our own strength. We don't have the required strength in ourselves. We need only give thanks and pray for the insight into God's answer to our situation.

When the apostle Paul wrote to the Corinthians, he didn't say that God sometimes or occasionally caused us to triumph. He said that our Lord *always* causes us to triumph *in Christ*. We need not even *feel* triumphant. We are, by virtue of Christ, a triumphant people, victorious in all that enters into our life. Thanks be to God!

"The riches of His free grace cause me daily to triumph
over all the temptations of the wicked one, who is very
vigilant, and seeks all occasions to disturb me."

GEORGE WHITEFIELD

OUR DEFEATED ENEMY

Be sober, be vigilant; because your adversary
the devil, as a roaring lion, walketh about,
seeking whom he may devour.

1 PETER 5:8

Our daily triumph (thanks be to God!) is not just over troubling circumstances. We who trust in Christ have a relentless enemy—a roaring lion—constantly searching for ways to rob us of our triumphant spirit, seeking whom he may devour. We must not allow him any entrance into our lives. We must always maintain the stance of resistance to the enemy of our souls.

Tonight, ready yourself for tomorrow—not by worrying, but by being vigilant, planting your feet on the solid ground of triumph. Satan must have no room, nor any sense of compromise on your part. Be diligent, be firm, and expect the enemy to flee as God enforces your resistance.

"Obey God in all things today! Drive out the enemy!
Lay the ax to the root of the tree, and the capacity
for Jesus Christ will be increased tomorrow."

ALAN REDPATH

FILLED!

Be not drunk with wine, wherein is excess;
but be filled with the Spirit.

EPHESIANS 5:18

What God wants in these troubling days is an army of ready, Spirit-filled soldiers ablaze with love and a fierce hatred of sin. Are you on fire today? If not, are you *willing* to be on fire? The kindling is already arranged, and the match can be struck at any time we choose. It all happens when we are "filled with the Spirit."

This filling of the Spirit is not an emotional response; it's a decision to be firmly Christ-centered in our thoughts and thus in our every action. It's a surrender of self and, by faith, an appropriation of the power of the Spirit.

We are to be soldiers of love, radiating joy and serving with devotion. Ablaze for God!

> *"Spirit filled souls are ablaze for God. They love with*
> *a love that glows. They serve with a faith that kindles.*
> *They serve with a devotion that consumes. They hate*
> *sin with fierceness that burns. They rejoice with a joy*
> *that radiates. Love is perfected in the fire of God."*
>
> **SAMUEL CHADWICK**

STILL FULL!

And to know the love of Christ, which passeth knowledge,
that ye might be filled with all the fulness of God.

EPHESIANS 3:19

To be a Spirit-filled Christian is to be filled with the fullness of God. That might sound as if it's a provision only for the super-spiritual saints who ponder the deep thoughts of God.

But no. *All* Christians are to be Spirit filled and are expected to walk daily in the Spirit.

Even as we rest from the day's labor, we experience the peace of Christ about us. We know by faith the love of Christ that passes even knowledge.

Many Christians are content to sit on the sidelines and await heaven. These people miss out on the wonderful Spirit-filled life they could have now.

If you want to experience peace, love, and joy, this life is for you. The same promises that are enjoyed by the "super-spiritual" saints are yours also.

"The Spirit-filled life is not a special, deluxe edition of Christianity.
It is part and parcel of the total plan of God for His people."

A.W. TOZER

THE JOY OF CREATING

Them hath he filled with wisdom of heart, to work all manner
of work, of the engraver, and of the cunning workman, and
of the embroiderer, in blue, and in purple, in scarlet, and
in fine linen, and of the weaver, even of them that do
any work, and of those that devise cunning work.

EXODUS 35:35

God endows each of us with certain creative gifts, just as in the Old Testament He gave some the gifts of furnishing the Tabernacle. Have you discovered your creative gifts? Every believer is created in the image of God and thus is also creative. Some Christians never uncover the latent talents God has given them, and others may misuse the gifts of God.

Today, consider your gifts. Consider how your abilities can reflect on God's creativity. The time for keeping your gifts buried or underused is long past. The world awaits a display of the God-given gifts within you. Whether your gift is music, art, literature, sculpting, sewing, building, or any of a thousand other gifts—it was given to you for a reason.

"Time is lost when we have not lived a full human
life, time unenriched by experience, creative
endeavor, enjoyment, and suffering."

DIETRICH BONHOEFFER

THE FRUIT OF CREATION

*The LORD spake unto Moses, saying, See, I have called by
name Bezaleel the son of Uri, the son of Hur, of the tribe
of Judah: And I have filled him with the spirit of God,
in wisdom, and in understanding, and in knowledge,
and in all manner of workmanship, to devise cunning
works, to work in gold, and in silver, and in brass,
and in cutting of stones, to set them, and in carving
of timber, to work in all manner of workmanship.*

EXODUS 31:1-5

God loves beauty. To see photos taken of faraway galaxies, to visit a beach at sunset, or to witness the birth of a child, we're confronted with the works of the Master Designer. And the wonder of it all is that He includes us as co-creators as we develop our creative talents. Tonight is a night to worship God as Creator and as the giver of your creative gifts. Pray specifically about how He might use your creativity. Let all your creative endeavors for God flow from your life of prayer—the true foundation of your gifts.

*"The greatest and best talent that God gives to any man
or woman in this world is the talent of prayer."*

ALEXANDER WHYTE

EVERY DAY A PRAYER DAY

Pray without ceasing.
1 THESSALONIANS 5:17

If you would have a good day, you must first unlock the door to God's will with the key of faith as you pray. A morning without prayer is like sending a boat to sea without a rudder. You may not know the course for the boat, but prayer sets the Lord as captain of the vessel. He will see us across today's seas and safely back to our harbor home at day's end. Though you may encounter the unexpected today, God will not be caught off guard. He holds the rudder steady whether the waves be calm or stormy.

How your day will unfold and come to a close may be determined by the prayers of the morning. As you pray, take time to praise God and to listen for His voice.

"The prayer offered to God in the morning during your quiet time is the key that unlocks the door of the day. Any athlete knows that it is the start that ensures a good finish."
ADRIAN ROGERS

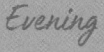

Prayer Tonight

*It came to pass in those days, that he went out into a
mountain to pray, and continued all night in prayer to God.*

Luke 6:12

Few of us make all-night prayer sessions a regular part of our spiritual life. But Jesus surely did. As important as morning prayer is, so too is evening prayer. It's a good time to review the events of the day, to consider any challenges to be faced, and, of course, to praise God for His presence throughout our daytime hours.

A concluding prayer might be for tomorrow, that during our sleeping hours God may prepare the events for the day ahead. Or perhaps your need is relational. Some relationships may need sorting out. Some need strengthening. Yet others need affirmation. But no matter the focus of your prayer, pray with a faith-filled heart.

Let's not neglect a visit to the prayer closet as we prepare for bed, so though we slumber, our prayer life remains vibrant.

*"The spirit of prayer has slumbered among us. The closet has
been too little frequented and delighted in. We have allowed
business, study or active labor to interfere with our closet-hours.
And the feverish atmosphere in which both the church and the
nation are enveloped has found its way into our prayer closets."*

Andrew Bonar

GOD'S FAITHFULNESS IN ADVERSITY

We are troubled on every side, yet not distressed;
we are perplexed, but not in despair; persecuted,
but not forsaken; cast down, but not destroyed.

2 CORINTHIANS 4:8-9

How often have we prayed earnestly for an end to a painful circumstance, only to see the situation remain the same or become even worse? "Where is God?" we may ask. "Why doesn't He answer? Why must this adversity continue?"

Often God's answer is that the circumstance was sent to change us, not for us to change the circumstance. In allowing the situation to remain unresolved, He allows it to continue to do its work. Paul was "troubled on every side." He was perplexed, persecuted, and cast down. But he also reports that he was not distressed or in despair, not forsaken or destroyed. We can rest assured that the same will be true for us. We will come out on the other side in victory and with a stronger faith when the trial has done its work.

"Every trial you meet with, every trouble you pass through,
and all the temptations you experience serve to confirm
the truth of God's Word; and if rightly viewed, and
properly improved, would strengthen your faith."

JAMES SMITH

SUSTAINING FAITH

O love the LORD, all ye his saints:
for the LORD preserveth the faithful.
PSALM 31:23

When touched by adversity, we can know—we *must* know—that God will sustain us and preserve us from the evil intent in the situation. The path through life is full of ups and downs, curves and straightaways. Our task is to learn to maneuver through the journey successfully. We do this by sustaining faith. We do this by absolute surrender to the working of God in our life. Those ups and downs, curves and straightaways are set by God. He will always lead us along the right way—if we will but trust. The destination is worth the often perilous journey. So, during the straightaways, rejoice and be glad. On the curves and in the valleys, hang tight and pray it through.

"[God] will lead you by a right way, though it may be by a
way of hardship, and crosses, and losses, and privations, to
the city of God. Oh! the blessedness of thus lying passive
in the hands of God, saying 'Undertake for me God!'"
JOHN MACDUFF

GLORIFYING GOD

I will praise thee, O Lord my God, with all my heart:
and I will glorify thy name for evermore.

PSALM 86:12

Glorifying God is one way of enjoying God. A faith that does not result in enjoying God is not the faith to which we're called. When we praise God with our whole heart, when we determine that come what may, we will glorify His name forever, we are released from many of life's woes. Why? Because our desire to glorify Him perfectly aligns with His desire for us. When we glorify God with our life, we find that *we* are the ones being blessed. God has so designed it.

Today, as the day begins, offer praise with your whole heart. Glorify His name today—and forevermore.

"Ardent love or desire introduced, as passionately longing to
please and glorify the Divine Being, to be in every respect
conformed to him, and in that way to enjoy him."

DAVID BRAINERD

IN MY LIFE

Let your light so shine before men,
that they may see your good works,
and glorify your Father which is in heaven.

MATTHEW 5:16

One way we glorify God is to do good works, thus allowing our light to shine before others. But make no mistake: The glory belongs to the Lord, never to us. The good works are a testament of God's presence in our life—and should serve as an invitation to others to join us in glorifying our Father in heaven.

What are your good works? They may very well begin tomorrow with the next need you encounter. God is best glorified by the good works we do for others. When we serve the needs of those around us, we're serving Christ.

"We are told to let our light shine, and if it does, we won't
need to tell anybody it does. Lighthouses don't fire cannons
to call attention to their shining—they just shine."

D.L. MOODY

FEAR NOT!

The LORD is on my side; I will not fear:
what can man do unto me?

PSALM 118:6

Fear lurks around our lives, seeking a way to find entrance. For when we fear, we're actively doubting God's care for us. The psalmist was wise to recognize that God was on his side—and we do well to recall that He is also on our side.

Nothing man can do to us can derail us from the tracks of God's will. No strategy of the enemy will prevail over us. God plans our every circumstance and arranges all things to work for our good. Why then could we possibly fear? Trust in the God whose eyes are upon us—the God who hears our prayers and secures His promises to us.

"If the Lord be with us, we have no cause of fear. His eye
is upon us, His arm over us, His ear open to our prayer;
His grace sufficient, His promise unchangeable."

JOHN NEWTON

THE ONE TRUE FEAR

The fear of the LORD tendeth to life:
and he that hath it shall abide satisfied;
he shall not be visited with evil.

PROVERBS 19:23

There is one fear that every believer must cultivate: fear of the Lord. Though some maintain that fearing God is simply an Old Testament directive, we find nowhere in the New Testament that we can now abandon the fear of the Lord. Properly understand, the fear of the Lord keeps us from many evils. This fear "tendeth to life," offering us a satisfied life and an escape from evil. Never diminish the need to fear God in your life. This fear comes with a promise of satisfaction.

"He who is governed by the fear of the Lord enjoys heart-
felt satisfaction; and the joys that spring from it are not
like the short-lived joys of the world, which die away into
sadness and misery; they last through life, they are vigorous
in old age, when the pleasures of sense have lost their
relish, and they triumph over death and all its terrors."

GEORGE LAWSON

PONDERING THE LOVE OF GOD

*Behold, what manner of love the Father hath
bestowed upon us, that we should be called the
sons of God: therefore the world knoweth
us not, because it knew him not.*

1 JOHN 3:1

The love God has for each of us is an anchor for the soul. Every day, we should take time to ponder this endless love that joins us to God's family as His sons and daughters. This love is not like human love—at least not in degrees. It far surpasses what little we know of love. Thus John could ask us to behold a manner of love that the world cannot know. Today is a day to keep God's love at the forefront of our thoughts. Ponder this love and find healing for your soul.

*"A habit of devout and thankful meditation upon the love
of God, as manifested in the sacrifice of Jesus Christ, and the
consequent gift of the Divine Spirit, joined with the humble,
thankful conviction that I am a child of God thereby, lies at
the foundation of all vigorous and happy Christian life."*

ALEXANDER MACLAREN

RESTING IN THE SAVING LOVE OF GOD

The LORD thy God in the midst of thee is mighty;
he will save, he will rejoice over thee with joy; he will
rest in his love, he will joy over thee with singing.

ZEPHANIAH 3:17

What does the love of God do for us? It changes us from the inside out. His love—at great expense—saves us from the penalty of our sins and from the power of sin. His love redeems our troubles so that what was designed to work against us now becomes an avenue for God's blessing. As we power down from our day, let's rest in the saving love of God.

"The Lord Jesus is not only a Savior—but he is 'mighty to save.'
He saves from sin. He delivers out of trouble. He redeems us
from the hands of our enemies. He has delivered his people
in all ages; he delivers them now, and he will deliver them
until deliverance is no longer needed. It cannot be wrong to
trust in him, for it is impossible for him to fail us, his word is
promised, his heart is in the work, and he gets great glory by it."

JAMES SMITH

FAVOR!

*Remember me, O LORD, with the favor that thou
bearest unto thy people: O visit me with thy salvation.*

PSALM 106:4

Make no mistake, Christians are no better than anyone else. We *are*, however, *better off* than many others. Why? Because we can enjoy favor from God. Our Father in heaven loves to bestow good gifts upon His children—and one of those gifts is favor.

By faith, we can count on God's favor in many aspects of our lives, including our careers, finances, and relationships, for instance. We must never take God's favor for granted, but we shortchange ourselves if we ignore this aspect of being one of God's children. After all, don't we favor our own children? How much more, then, does God favor His children.

Today, look for God's favor in your life. Expect it.

*"From his favor flows every good and perfect gift. To
be God's favorite is an honor indeed! If God blesses
graciously, he looks for no reason in the creature why
he should bless—but he does so gratuitously."*

JAMES SMITH

FAVOR WITH GOD

His anger endureth but a moment; in his favor
is life: weeping may endure for a night,
but joy cometh in the morning.

PSALM 30:5

Sometimes life makes us weary. Perhaps this evening finds you so. In your hours of evening rest, look up and see God's favor operating in your life. For "in his favor is life." We need not look far to see the results of God's favor. But if we are in a rough patch right now, we can ask for God's favor to be upon us in the trial.

God's favor, like all His gifts, is only received by faith. If you do not see favor in your life, remember that we walk not by sight but by faith.

Let faith bring favor more fully into your life.

"'In His favor is life'; and to be without this favor is to be
unhappy here, and to be shut out from joy hereafter. There
is no life worthy of the name of life except that which flows
from His assured friendship. Without that friendship, our life
here is a burden and a weariness; but with that friendship
we fear no evil, and all sorrow is turned into joy."

HORATIUS BONAR

SAFETY

The horse is prepared against the day of battle:
but safety is of the LORD.
PROVERBS 21:31

When we face difficulty, we may well prepare for the battle with an expectation of winning. But for believers in Christ, our safety—our victory—is of the Lord, not of ourselves. Many times we engage the battle ourselves, only to suffer setbacks or even defeat. Placing trust in oneself during a fierce battle dooms us to lose the fight.

No matter how well our "horse" is prepared for battle, unless the Lord fights for us, we will suffer loss.

As you recount God's blessings today, make the promise of safety near the top of the list. Yes, prepare the horse, but trust in God.

"In Jesus Christ on the Cross there is refuge; there is
safety; there is shelter; and all the power of sin upon
our track cannot reach us when we have taken
shelter under the Cross that atones for our sins."

A.C. DIXON

DWELLING IN SAFETY

I will both lay me down in peace, and sleep:
for thou, LORD, only makest me dwell in safety.

PSALM 4:8

Tonight you will dwell in safety. God so orders it. You are under His watchful eye and may therefore lay down in peaceful sleep. As you retire, meditate on the promises of God for you. But don't just name them—*ponder* them. Consider the implication for your life. Pray the promises back to God. Select an issue facing you now, and instead of worrying about it, find the right promise to stand on. Then meditate on God's promise, not on your circumstance.

His Word is so full of precious promises that you will lay down in peace and surely drift off in only minutes. And your sleep will be sweet.

"They slumber sweetly whom faith rocks to sleep. No pillow so soft as a promise; no cover so warm as an assured interest in Christ."

CHARLES SPURGEON

GOD'S GOOD GIFTS

Every good gift and every perfect gift is from above,
and cometh down from the Father of lights, with whom
is no variableness, neither shadow of turning.

JAMES 1:17

His role as gift giver is one of God's permanent attributes. It's His very nature to give good and perfect gifts to His children. In this, there is no variableness or shadow of turning.

Today, be aware of the gifts He is giving you now. Call to mind the gifts of the past. Remember that God is the true source of every good and perfect gift. Anticipate with gratitude the gifts of the future—not just temporal gifts but also gifts of mercy, grace, and favor.

If you have the opportunity, speak to someone else about the gifts of God. If you see a need you can meet for someone else, be a channel of God's blessing for that person.

"God is the fountain of all our mercies—temporal, spiritual, and
eternal. Whatever may be the streams, he is the Source! Whatever
may be the instruments to promote his designs, he is the Agent!"

WILLIAM NICHOLSON

UNSPEAKABLE LOVE

Thanks be unto God for his unspeakable gift.

2 CORINTHIANS 9:15

If we were required to name our favorite gift from God, I suspect we'd all choose His unspeakable love. For out of His love flow all the other gifts.

This love is unspeakable because of its greatness. It's like trying to define the undefinable. God's love, like the universe, is infinite. When we think His love has surely been exhausted, we see fresh evidence of this limitless love. The truth is, we can never fully realize the depths of God's unspeakable love on this side of eternal life—but we can receive that love with gratitude. We can consider the cross of Christ as the prime example of this ineffable divine love.

What comfort it is to end another day with an awareness that God's love has been our companion throughout the morning and afternoon hours. And even now, this very evening, God's constant love remains with us, upon us, and unspeakably in us.

"We are never nearer Christ than when we find ourselves lost in a holy amazement at His unspeakable love."

JOHN OWEN

UNIQUELY US

I will praise thee; for I am fearfully and wonderfully made.
PSALM 139:14

We all understand that no two snowflakes are alike. Nor do any two people share a fingerprint. But God's design for each of us goes much deeper than our fingers. From head to toe, inside and out, you are uniquely *you*. In creating us, God didn't just throw together the various parts that make up each person. He designed each of us as if we were to be His only created being. Yes, we're that special. Our very souls should cry out in gratitude for our life. We were made to be part of history. We are each part of God's eternal plan. Thus we join the psalmist in praising God for including us.

> *"The soul is the glory of the creation. The soul is a beam of God.... There is in the soul, an idea and resemblance of God, an analogy of similitude of God. If David so admired the rare texture and workmanship of his body, if the cabinet is so curiously wrought, what is the jewel! How richly and gloriously the soul is embroidered! It is divinely inlaid and enameled. The body is but the sheath."*
>
> THOMAS WATSON

A WELL-DESIGNED LIFE

The steps of a good man are ordered by the LORD:
and he delighteth in his way.

PSALM 37:23

God created each of us uniquely. But He didn't stop there. Just as He created us, He also created a plan for us—a destiny to fulfill. When we rebel or ignore that plan, we wander aimlessly with little meaning attached to our existence. But when we discern God's path for us and walk in it consistently, we "delighteth" in our way.

Your steps today were ordered by the Lord. So will be tomorrow's steps. Be thankful and stay on the path.

"The earthly parent, after a few brief years, leaves the child
to its own resources, to walk alone, and care for itself. Not
so our Heavenly Father. The man's footsteps, as well as
the child's, are 'ordered.' In all the varied circumstances
of existence, the Eternal God is still his refuge…and as
he pursues his onward way, at times ready to faint, ready
to fall—stumbling along the rough, stony path—his
cry is never unaided, his prayer never unanswered."

JOHN MACDUFF

GRACE AND MORE GRACE

*He giveth more grace. Wherefore he saith, God
resisteth the proud, but giveth grace unto the humble.*

JAMES 4:6

God's grace is a lifelong need for all of us. In truth, we will never outgrow the need for "more grace." As today begins, look to a fresh supply of the Lord's grace, saved especially for you. Whether your day holds rain or sunshine, claim God's grace. If mistakes abound, if sin assaults, if forgiveness is necessary, all you need is found in God's supply of grace. Never fear that He will run out of grace for you. Instead, rest in the knowledge that we each have a "grace account" in God's supply depot that will never run out.

*"You find by experience that you must have grace for every
moment—more grace—fresh grace—abounding grace. The
battle of yesterday must be fought again today. The race of today,
must be run again tomorrow. Fellow-pilgrim, there is no rest
for you while here in this poor world! You must fight, and fight
again; run, and run again, looking to Jesus. Fear not! God
will uphold you. He will uphold you according to His word."*

GEORGE MYLNE

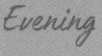
MERCY AND GRACE
IN OUR TIME OF NEED

Let us therefore come boldly unto the throne of grace,
that we may obtain mercy, and find
grace to help in time of need.

HEBREWS 4:16

When we think of entering God's presence, seldom do we see ourselves doing so "boldly." We think, "Me? Approach the throne of grace boldly? I don't think so!"

And yet what do we find when we dare to believe God's Word and come to His throne of grace? We find mercy and grace for our time of need. When we no longer need mercy and grace, then we no longer need to approach that divine throne. In other words, we must never allow ourselves to think we no longer need to approach Him boldly.

"What a multitude of eyes and hearts wait at the Throne of
Grace! He has a numerous and necessitous family, but He is
rich enough to supply them all. And His tender compassions
extend to the poorest and most unworthy of them! Like
the sun, He can cheer and enlighten millions of His poor
pensioners at once! He gives to each one as bountifully—
as if there were no others to partake of His favor!"

JOHN NEWTON

OUR 24/7 GOD

Behold, he that keepeth Israel
shall neither slumber nor sleep.

PSALM 121:4

We awake—sometimes very slowly!—and begin a new day. But God was up way before us. In fact, God was up all night brooding over us with His watchful eye. Our Father is a 24/7 parent. He knows that our enemies are many and that they have designs to make us falter or fail. But God upholds us against all the enemies and struggles confronting us. He never relaxes His watch over us. Every time we face an obstacle, if we only listen closely, we'll hear Him whisper, "I will take care of you." He's that kind of parent.

"The believer often moves on slippery ground. Various enemies, also, dash against him. Left to himself, how quickly will he fall! But the Lord upholds him, so he stands as a rock against the lashing billows. The care which preserves him never relaxes its watchful guardianship. The eyes of the Lord, through day and night, from the opening to the closing of the year, are fixed immovably on His waiting people."

HENRY LAW

GOD OF THE NIGHT WATCH

When thou liest down, thou shalt not be afraid:
yea, thou shalt lie down, and thy sleep shall be sweet.

PROVERBS 3:24

How sweet is the sleep of the Christian who trusts in God. We lay our head on our pillow tonight with a sigh of contentment, remembering that God has spent the day with us, overseeing all that pertains to us. He has been at our side all day and is now alert to our every need and desire. We never grow old enough to no longer need a heavenly Father to care for us.

Contrast our peaceful repose with the troubled sleep of those who take their problems and worries to bed with them.

Tonight we have nothing to fear, for we serve the God of the night watch.

"He who follows Christ's footsteps will tread surely, and not fear
foes. Quiet repose in hours of rest will be his. A day filled with
happy service will be followed by a night full of calm slumber."

ALEXANDER MACLAREN

GENEROSITY

The liberal soul shall be made fat:
and he that watereth shall be watered also himself.

PROVERBS 11:25

Those in need around us are Christ in disguise. When we give to those who need what we have (money, time, affirmation), we are giving to Christ. And if we ever ask why God has entrusted us with more than we need, we must realize that these blessings have been given to us so we can be a channel of God's care for the needy. God sees. He will be in debt to no one. When we give, He will find a way to repay.

Never begrudge giving. Giving is God's nature, and because we are filled with His Spirit, it is also now our nature. Who, then, can you "water" today?

"There is nothing lost by relieving the needy. An estate may be
imparted yet not impaired. The flowers yield honey to the bee,
yet do not hurt their own fruit. When the candle of prosperity
shines upon us, we may light our neighbor who is in the dark,
and have never the less light ourselves. Whatever is disbursed
to pious uses, God brings it back to us some other way."

THOMAS WATSON

THE GIFT OF RECEIVING

Peter saith unto him, Thou shalt never wash my feet.
Jesus answered him, If I wash thee not,
thou hast no part with me.

JOHN 13:8

Giving is our new nature. But are we also able to receive? If we have needs that others want to meet, are we tempted to turn them away out of pride or perhaps because we don't want to consider ourselves in someone else's debt?

Such an attitude is not of Christ. He would have us give liberally but also be humble enough to receive. Peter rebuffed Jesus's desire to wash his feet...until Jesus told him that unless He could wash his feet, he could have no part with Jesus. So, too, for us: If we cannot freely receive ministry from God, neither can we freely give it.

"If you want to know the blessedness of giving you must begin
with knowing the blessedness of receiving. Cast away all
indifference and unbelief and doubt and receive in humble faith
all that God has to give you... Then you will be prepared to give,
because you will have the spirit of your Master guiding you."

GEORGE EVERARD

THE GUARDIAN OF TIME

*My times are in thy hand: deliver me from the hand
of mine enemies, and from them that persecute me.*

PSALM 31:15

A life surrendered to God is a life that worries not about time. Our times are in God's hands. Our day of birth was in His plan, as will be the day of our death and every day in between those two events.

Time is a resource—one of God's many gifts to us. We are to use it wisely and not squander it. But the hours of life placed in the hands of God will find time for every duty He has called you to. And plenty of time to rest and relax too. How is your time today? Rushed? Easy? No matter, for given to the Lord, your day will be orchestrated by God, the ultimate timekeeper.

*"Thank God that your times, your interests, your salvation, are
all out of your hands, and out of the hands of all creatures,
supremely and safely in his. Forward in the path of duty,
of labor, and of suffering. Aim to resemble Christ more
closely in your disposition, your spirit, your whole life."*

OCTAVIUS WINSLOW

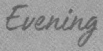
REDEEM THE TIME

*Walk in wisdom toward them that are
without, redeeming the time.*
COLOSSIANS 4:5

Though our times are in God's hands, He has made us stewards of our days and hours and years. We must treasure the gift of time and, like money, budget our use of our hours. Many of us could easily remove some time wasters from our days. We could perhaps entrust certain job-related matters to someone less busy. Home chores could also be delegated. But the hardest decision may be identifying the ways we squander our time. Watching too much TV? Browsing too many websites?

Here's a test: Do you find yourself putting prayer and God's Word so far down on your to-do list that days often pass without your taking quality time to commune with God?

*"No man ever rose to eminence who did not wisely employ
his time. The student economizes every moment and never
tires in his researches. The philosopher tests by science and
reason the mysteries of nature, omitting no opportunity
or detail. And thus the statesman studies the complicated
problems of politics and provides for their solution in season
and out. And so the Christian student, the eyes of whose
understanding are opened, ponders Divine truth."*

J.G. ANGLEY

PRECIOUS MEMORIES

Mary kept all these things, and pondered them in her heart.

LUKE 2:19

A good memory can be a blessing or a curse. Fond memories allow us to revisit happy times and be thankful to God. Sad memories serve a purpose too. They remind us that God has brought us through trials before, and when fresh trials arise, He will bring us through again.

Mary pondered the events in her life as the magnitude of God's use of her and her Son unfolded before her eyes. Similarly, God is unfolding your future, day by day. Every "today" is relevant in God's plan. Don't mistake the day's events as mere happenstance. Some things that seem insignificant now may be remembered as greatly important in light of future events. Other things that trouble us today may be dismissed entirely tomorrow. Some things may need to be recalled with a fresh offering of thankfulness. God wastes nothing.

"My memory is nearly gone; but I remember two things; That I am a great sinner, and that Christ is a great Savior."

JOHN NEWTON

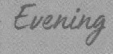

NEW MEMORIES

I have received of the Lord that which also I delivered unto
you, that the Lord Jesus the same night in which he was
betrayed took bread: and when he had given thanks, he
brake it, and said, Take, eat: this is my body, which is
broken for you: this do in remembrance of me. After the
same manner also he took the cup, when he had supped,
saying, this cup is the new testament in my blood: this
do ye, as oft as ye drink it, in remembrance of me.

1 Corinthians 11:23-25

Memory is important to God. That's one reason He instituted what we call communion, the Lord's Supper, or the Eucharist. In partaking of the bread and the cup, we're reminded of the price paid for our sins. And though we usually celebrate this memorial event on a Sunday, it's important to daily recall and ponder the gift at great cost. As we remember Him, may we also call out as did the thief on the cross, "Lord, remember me!"

"When these failing lips grow dumb,
And thought and memory flee;
When you shall in your kingdom come,
Jesus, remember me!"

James Montgomery

OUR PROMISE KEEPER

*This is the promise that he hath
promised us, even eternal life.*
1 JOHN 2:25

Our Christian faith is built on the solid promises of God. Eternal life, for instance, is promised to all who believe in Christ and receive Him as Savior. The certainty of our salvation is no small matter. If this very vital promise is invalid, all other promises of God are in doubt. But praise God, the promises *are* valid. Why? Because of the One behind the promises. God cannot lie. What He says, He means. What He promises, He fulfills. We never have need to doubt our eternal home. The Lord has secured our happiness here on earth and our everlasting joy throughout all eternity. Such knowledge makes waiting with anticipation all the easier.

*"To be assured of our salvation is no arrogant stoutness. It is
faith. It is devotion. It is not presumption. It is God's promise."*
AUGUSTINE

PROMISES KEPT

All the promises of God in him are yea,
and in him Amen, unto the glory of God by us.

2 CORINTHIANS 1:20

As evening is upon us, it does us good to reflect on the promises of God. Perhaps today you saw a promise fulfilled. For every day God is keeping His word, all to our benefit. Consider that God may have worked behind the scenes to bring about the fulfillment of a promise without you even noticing.

Wise are the Christians who build their lives on the promises of God, who enjoy the promises they see fulfilled and are grateful for the unseen promises fulfilled.

Happy are the Christians whose one desire is to know more fully the great Promise Keeper. Blessed are those who can laugh at impossibilities.

With God, we are secure. We have His promise to hear and answer our prayers, a promise that trumps even those things that seem impossible.

Rest well tonight, giving thanks to God for His abundant promises.

"Faith, mighty faith, the promise sees, and looks to that alone;
Laughs at impossibilities, and cries: It shall be done!"

CHARLES WESLEY

GLORIFYING GOD IN OUR FEW SHORT YEARS

*What is your life? It is even a vapor, that
appeareth for a little time, and then vanisheth away.*

JAMES 4:14

It doesn't take long to leave our mark for the Lord in this vapor-like life. David Brainerd was a missionary to Native Americans, yet he was struck down by consumption at age twenty-nine. He would be astonished at the impact his journals have had. He is now recognized as one of the most influential Christians of the nineteenth century.

Betsie ten Boom was a quiet woman, tending to bookkeeping for her father…until she and her sister, Corrie, were arrested and taken to Ravensbrück concentration camp, where she would eventually die. And yet her influence on Corrie set in motion events that neither could have imagined (read their story in *The Hiding Place*).

We never know how God wants to use us. But we must allow His will in our lives, whether short or long.

*"We should always look upon ourselves as God's servants,
placed in God's world, to do his work; and accordingly labor
faithfully for him; not with a design to grow rich and great,
but to glorify God, and do all the good we possibly can."*

DAVID BRAINERD

HE IS WORTHY

*Worthy is the Lamb that was slain to receive
power, and riches, and wisdom, and strength,
and honor, and glory, and blessing.*

REVELATION 5:12

Evening is the perfect time to set aside some quiet moments for intimate praise and worship to God. The work of the day is done. We can give thanks. We can pray for things we anticipate for tomorrow. But perhaps the best part of worship is simply praising God for who He is. In praise, we can declare Him worthy, affirm His majesty, and contemplate His love.

Every person will have their own way of expressing praise. And when that homage comes from the innocent heart of a believer, there are no wrong words, no inept ways of praising. Best of all, we find that praising God enables us to enjoy being in His presence.

Glorify God tonight with your praises.

*"If you had a thousand crowns you should put them all on
the head of Christ! And if you had a thousand tongues
they should all sing his praise, for he is worthy!"*

WILLIAM TIPTAFT

REPENTANCE

Despisest thou the riches of his goodness and
forbearance and longsuffering; not knowing that the
goodness of God leadeth thee to repentance?

ROMANS 2:4

The Christian life is a repentant life. In response to the Holy Spirit's conviction of sin in our lives, we readily repent and appropriate the forgiveness offered us in Christ.

Repentance is a turning around. A change of direction. While we once enjoyed certain activities and amusements, we now regard them as roadblocks to the joyous Christian life.

Listen today for the Spirit's urging toward repentance. Consider anything that weakens your appreciation for the love of God as something from which you need to repent.

Never forget that repentance isn't a negative decision; it's a positive one. The things from which we must repent are not healthy for us. To let them go is to break free and move forward. In true repentance, the thing repented of will not be missed for long.

"The love of God is the most powerful persuasive to repentance."

WILLIAM BATES

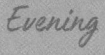

Keeping Clear with God

If we confess our sins, he is faithful and just to forgive us our sins, and to cleanse us from all unrighteousness.

1 John 1:9

To become a Christian is to repent. But repentance doesn't end there. Repentance is necessary whenever we give in to the sinful thoughts and activities that limit us from being the person God created us to be.

Repentance is nothing to fear. Repentance is a clean break from our chains. When we become aware of sin, confession and repentance enable us to appropriate the forgiveness that is already ours in Christ.

End each day with a reckoning with your conscience. Does it convict you of any known sin? By this daily reckoning, we keep short accounts with God.

"Repentance is a grace, and must have its daily operation, as well as other graces. A true penitent must go on from faith to faith, from strength to strength; he must never stand still or turn back. True repentance is a continued spring, where the waters of godly sorrow are always flowing."

Thomas Brooks

THE GIFT OF FRIENDSHIP

A friend loveth at all times,
and a brother is born for adversity.
PROVERBS 17:17

There are many things in life that are shadows of God's truth. For instance, the love of friends is a shadowlike version of God's love for us. Friendship reminds us of affection, affirmation, and, perhaps most of all, commitment.

What is a friend without a commitment to stay by our side through thick and thin? That commitment, too, can be likened to God's commitment to us. In the person of the Holy Spirit, God is our "helper." In the person of Jesus Christ, He is our true brother. In His role as our Father, God is our protector. In every way possible, friendship on earth is but a shadow of the friendship of heaven.

Who, on earth, is your closest friend? Pray for them today and, if possible, call or email to thank them for their friendship.

"The dearest friend on earth is a mere
shadow compared to Jesus Christ."
OSWALD CHAMBERS

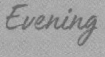
NEW FRIENDS AND OLD

Greater love hath no man than this,
that a man lay down his life for his friends.

JOHN 15:13

Who among us does not desire an unbreakable friendship? A friendship that would even suffer death in the place of the befriended. That's the friendship God offers every human being.

Yes, such a bonding is expensive. Jesus tells us we must surrender all to be His friend. But for those who take Him up on His offer, we find that the price is cheap compared to the benefits.

Friendship with God is the pinnacle of all friendships. End your day with a word of thanks to the Friend who has laid down His life for you.

> *"No matter how low down you are; no matter what your*
> *disposition has been; you may be low in your thoughts,*
> *words, and actions; you may be selfish; your heart may*
> *be overflowing with corruption and wickedness; yet Jesus*
> *will have compassion upon you. He will speak comforting*
> *words to you; not treat you coldly or spurn you, as perhaps*
> *those of earth would, but will speak tender words, and*
> *words of love and affection and kindness…. He is a faithful*
> *friend—a friend that sticketh closer than a brother."*

D.L. MOODY

HE IS THE VINE

*I am the vine, ye are the branches: He that
abideth in me, and I in him, the same bringeth forth
much fruit: for without me ye can do nothing.*

JOHN 15:5

Who among us doesn't wish to bear "much fruit"? The key, as Jesus tells us, is to abide in Him…for without Him, we can do nothing. The conclusion is that all the good fruit we bear comes not from ourselves—our planning, our far-fetched ideas, or even our giving. All that comes from self amounts to nothing. Conversely, all the good that flows through us as life in the branches comes from the life in the vine. How much more fruit might we daily bear by continuing to abide in the vine—and that through faith?

*"Abide in Me says Jesus. Cling to Me. Stick fast to Me. Live
the life of close and intimate communion with Me. Get
nearer to Me. Roll every burden on Me. Cast your
whole weight on Me. Never let go your hold on Me for a
moment. Be, as it were, rooted and planted in Me. Do
this and I will never fail you. I will ever abide in you."*

J.C. RYLE

WE ARE THE BRANCHES

Abide in me, and I in you. As the branch cannot
bear fruit of itself, except it abide in the vine;
no more can ye, except ye abide in me.

JOHN 15:4

Make no mistake: God is doing a work in each of His believing children. Today may have seemed mundane, but no day abiding in Christ is without benefits. Branches don't appear on the vine suddenly. Rather, they grow as the vine imparts life to its farthest reaches.

We can choose the life of the vine—or we can choose to bear our own fruit with disappointing results. The only fruit the Father values is that which comes from the Son, who is the vine. If we, as branches, wish to honor God with the fruit we bear, we must abide in the true vine—the Lord Jesus Christ.

"Let man choose Life; let him daily nourish his soul; let him
forever starve the old life; let him abide continuously as a
living branch in the Vine, and the True-Vine Life will flow
into his soul, assimilating, renewing, conforming to Type,
till Christ, pledged by His own law, be formed in him."

HENRY DRUMMOND

FOUND IN CHRIST

Be found in him, not having mine own righteousness,
which is of the law, but that which is through the faith of Christ,
the righteousness which is of God by faith.

PHILIPPIANS 3:9

When we lay down our own claim to righteousness and take on ourselves the righteousness that is of God by faith, we are true Christians. To trust in our own works is deception and pride.

We may wrongly measure our righteousness by how we have kept God's law or even our own faulty laws of how things ought to be. There is only one righteous one in all creation—and that's Christ, our Lord. Any other claims to righteousness are worthless in God's eyes. Today, live not by your own standard of righteousness; instead, cling to Christ and claim His righteousness as your own.

"If our desires meet and center in Christ—we must be true
Christians. If to know Christ, to win Christ, to magnify Christ,
to be found in Christ, to be conformed to Christ, to be with
Christ, and rejoice in the day of Christ's second coming are the
desires of our souls then we are as really Christians as Paul was!"

JAMES SMITH

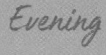

AN EXCHANGED LIFE

I am crucified with Christ: nevertheless I live; yet not I,
but Christ liveth in me: and the life which I now live
in the flesh I live by the faith of the Son of God,
who loved me, and gave himself for me.

GALATIANS 2:20

Paul knew the secret to life: his "self" being crucified with Christ and henceforth living by the faith of the Son of God. Some have called this the "exchanged life." We exchange our life for His life. We die, but we live on in the flesh because Christ lives in us. Other attempts to live the Christian life find us either failing entirely or becoming legalists—the very thing Christ came to save us from. Paul's secret is one that has been found by countless Christians down through the ages. Tonight, may that secret comfort us and give us courage to be the true Christians God has called us to be.

"The secret of Victory is simply Christ himself in
the heart of the believer. This truth, of Christ's
indwelling, is, and always has been, a mystery."

ROSALIND GOFORTH

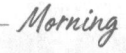
THE RIGHTEOUS GOD

The LORD is righteous in all his ways,
and holy in all his works.

PSALM 145:17

Today we can be thankful that God is righteous and holy in all His ways. To us, that translates as God is fair, never straying from the truth and always utterly beyond reproach. We are among His "works," and He is therefore "holy" in His dealings with us. He is above all, the righteous God.

To such a God we can boldly submit. We can honor this God through living by faith—the only path to knowing Him. We can also honor Him through being righteous in all *our* ways.

Every day the question confronts us: Am I trusting in self, or am I relying on Christ and Christ alone?

"This is faith: a renouncing of everything we are
apt to call our own and relying wholly upon the
blood, righteousness, and intercession of Jesus."

JOHN NEWTON

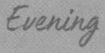

TRUSTING WHO GOD IS

Every word of God is pure: he is a shield
unto them that put their trust in him.

PROVERBS 30:5

Oh, the purity of God and His Word! How easy it is to trust in our Lord, who shields us from danger, who watches over us through the night and awakens us to a fresh new day. What, then, does He require of us in return for His gifts? *Simply faith.* And what *is* faith? It's believing God's Word and daily living it out in full trust of Him. The more we trust, the more we find that He is trustworthy. The more we have faith, the more we find that He is faithful. The more we give of ourselves, the more He gives of Himself.

Daily, we put our trust in many things—government, financial institutions, schools, our workplaces, our churches—but all these are as nothing when compared to trusting the God we cannot see.

"Christ will always accept the faith that puts its trust in Him."
ANDREW MURRAY

THE WORD OF GOD FOR TODAY

*For this cause also thank we God without ceasing,
because, when ye received the word of God which ye
heard of us, ye received it not as the word of men, but
as it is in truth, the word of God, which effectually
worketh also in you that believe.*

1 THESSALONIANS 2:13

The Bible is our lifeline. What we know of God, salvation, eternal life, even life itself, is found in God's Word. Many Christians are anemic because they don't get enough "iron" from knowing God's Word.

Reading the Word is fine, but it's not enough. Every growing believer must internalize God's Word—that's where changes in our life happen. That's where it "effectually worketh" in us.

Today, let the Word be your standard. It truly works in those who believe.

*"The Word of God I think of as a straight edge, which shows
up our own crookedness. We can't really tell how crooked our
thinking is until we line it up with the straight edge of Scripture."*

ELISABETH ELLIOT

THE WORD OF
GOD FOR TONIGHT

*These are they which are sown on good ground;
such as hear the word, and receive it, and bring forth fruit,
some thirtyfold, some sixty, and some an hundred.*

MARK 4:20

Internalizing God's Word begins with a love for His Word. When we love something, we delight in it. So too will we delight in God's Word as we come to love it. By receiving God's Word, we reap the harvest of the one who has sown good seed.

Do you want to bring forth fruit thirtyfold, sixtyfold, or even a hundredfold? Love God's Word, read it, meditate on it, internalize it…and tonight go to sleep with a favorite verse in your thoughts.

*"O, for greater love to the Scriptures—that we may know
them, enjoy them, conform to them, exercise faith in them,
and make them our delight! May we read them daily, pray
over them constantly, meditate on them frequently, and
manifest their holy tendency in life and death. May our
memories be stored with them, our hearts be sanctified
by them, and our lives correspond with them."*

JAMES SMITH

A Treasure Hunt

*The kingdom of heaven is like unto treasure
hid in a field; the which when a man hath found,
he hideth, and for joy thereof goeth and selleth
all that he hath, and buyeth that field.*

MATTHEW 13:44

Those who merely read or even study God's Word will find some benefit. But those who are willing to dig deeper will find a treasure. That treasure is the gospel in its fullest. The gospel—the "good news"—is more than just reserving a spot in heaven when we die.

There are aspects of the gospel that are hidden from the lost. Even many young believers are scarcely aware of the riches to be found in the field for which we would gladly sell all. At its root, the gospel is a gospel of joy. Pure joy. Expect that joy to be yours today.

*"The child of God is, from necessity, a joyful man. His sins are
forgiven, his soul is justified, his person is adopted, his trials
are blessings, his conflicts are victories, his death is immortality,
his future is a heaven of inconceivable, unthought of, untold,
and endless blessedness. With such a God, such a Savior, and
such a hope, is he not, ought he not, to be a joyful man?"*

OCTAVIUS WINSLOW

PONDERING THE TREASURE

*Yea, if thou criest after knowledge, and liftest up
thy voice for understanding; if thou seekest her as
silver, and searchest for her as for hid treasures;
then shalt thou understand the fear of the
LORD, and find the knowledge of God.*

PROVERBS 2:3-5

Earthly treasures abound. Many have sacrificed all to accumulate material wealth. Some seek hidden fortunes with the lottery or the roulette wheel. Others may seek hidden treasures with a metal detector. But an even greater detector of treasure is the Christian who digs through the Word seeking divine riches. Riches so valuable that even all the earth's gold and silver can't come near to its worth. And miracle of miracle—that treasure is *ours* and is given *freely*. To access this treasure, put aside the hunger for earthly treasure. Let Christ alone be your treasure. He will be enough.

*"You must keep all earthy treasures out of your heart, and let
Christ be your treasure, and let Him have your heart."*

CHARLES SPURGEON

THE LOVE OF THE WORLD

Love not the world, neither the things that are
in the world. If any man love the world,
the love of the Father is not in him.

1 JOHN 2:15

We all face a choice. Will we have what this world offers us… or will we choose Christ and the kingdom of God? We can't have both. The one is in direct opposition to the other. Never the twain shall meet. If we choose this world, we can never find what our heart seeks. In Christ alone will we find spiritual rest and fulfillment.

Today you may experience an attractive pull toward the world. Consider it seriously. Every believer must be fully convinced that he or she is giving up dross for gold. When a person chooses God's kingdom over this present world, God sees to it that there will be no disappointment with the choice.

"The two poles could sooner meet—than the love
of Christ and the love of the world."

RICHARD BAXTER

NOTHING TO GAIN

What shall it profit a man, if he shall gain
the whole world, and lose his own soul?

MARK 8:36

It's tragic to think of the men and women who have sought happiness only in this present world. When they're gone, their graves are much like that of the poorest soul—the holes in the ground look remarkably the same. If they have "gained the whole world," they have still lost the race. Their souls have chosen poorly.

Blessed—truly blessed—are those who see the emptiness of the world and choose instead to live this mortal life as ones who have eternal palaces awaiting in eternity.

> *"True Christian, a word for you: You know these things; you*
> *can say, 'By the grace of God I have been brought to see the*
> *emptiness of this world, and the value of my soul; by the*
> *grace of God I am what I am.' Oh, remember then,*
> *to make full proof that you are one of Christ's flock,*
> *by your daily conduct, your habits, your temper."*

J.C. RYLE

LOOK UP, NOT DOWN

My voice shalt thou hear in the morning,
O LORD; in the morning will I direct my
prayer unto thee, and will look up.

PSALM 5:3

Today is a day to look up, not down. Look up and see your triumphant life. See your victory over adversity, your brilliant future laid out for you by a loving heavenly Father. Christ suffered greatly, but He looked ahead and chose the cross for the glory beyond. Your trials today are below you. Don't look down at them. Victory comes by looking up. The answer to your prayers will come as God dispatches the angels to tend to you.

"Many of us go worrying all through this life, keeping our eyes
always downcast on the path we are treading. We see all the
troubles, the difficulties, and discouragements but we never raise
our eyes to see the joys and the eternal blessings which are waiting
for us. We ought to learn this life-secret, which made Christ
look past the shame and sorrow of His cross and see the glory
beyond. Learn to look up toward Heaven! Think of its joys and
its blessedness until earth's trials shall melt away in the brightness,
and its griefs and losses are forgotten in the hopes of eternal glory!"

J.R. MILLER

GENTLY AND GRADUALLY

Rest in the LORD, and wait patiently for him.

PSALM 37:7

As we look up to heaven and not down at our trials, we must train ourselves to be patient as God works. We need physical rest tonight, but for many the need for emotional rest from worry is equally strong. Christians who have grown through the trials of life can withstand future storms that will come. For them, experience has been a great teacher. Others may still be learning to accept God's timetable with patience. For them, experience is presently a great teacher. Trials are merely God's way of teaching us to rest in Him and to wait patiently for His gentle and gradual answer.

Patience is trust lived out, knowing the answer *will* come. God is not slow to act; we are simply quick to worry.

"God works powerfully, but for the most part gently and gradually."

JOHN NEWTON

SOUGHT BY GOD

We love him, because he first loved us.

1 John 4:19

The love of God for the sinner is such a perfect love that it simply must come first, before our love for Him.

God initiates a love relationship by seeking us out—and then we respond by returning that love. A love that would begin with us would be a faulty love, with no object or emotion to respond to. Our love for God comes as we perceive and receive His love for us.

Today, meditate on the fact that God has chosen you to be an object of His divine love. It will put fire in your soul.

"He loves me, an insignificant nobody, full of sin who deserved to be in hell; who loves him so little in return. God loves me. Beloved believer, does not this melt you? Does not this fire your soul? I know it does if it is really believed. It must!"

Charles Spurgeon

PLEASING GOD

Without faith it is impossible to please him: for he
that cometh to God must believe that he is, and that he
is a rewarder of them that diligently seek him.

HEBREWS 11:6

Faith in God's love for us brings about our love for Him in return. We respond by seeking Him through faith—and then receiving the reward He grants to diligent seekers. If we be true Christians, we will not doubt His love. His promises will light our way through life. Doubt is our enemy, robbing us of trusting the One who is the most trustworthy.

"The more fully and constantly we trust Him, the more we walk
by faith, the more will the Lord delight in us. God is pleased
when we cling to Him in the darkness, look to Him for the
fulfilling of His promises, count upon His loving kindness. But
He is displeased when we doubt His Word or suspect His love.
Faith in God, in His precepts, in His promises, is the grand and
distinguishing principle which is to actuate all our conduct."

A.W. PINK

GOD'S GOOD PLEASURE

Fear not, little flock; for it is your Father's
good pleasure to give you the kingdom.
LUKE 12:32

It is not with reluctance that God gifts His children with the kingdom and all that accompanies it. He does so with "good pleasure."

God, in fact, awaits our petitions and eagerly grants those that are beneficial to us. All of this is our privilege while on earth. But consider that it will also be God's good pleasure to give us heavenly gifts throughout eternity. These are no doubt gifts that we can't even imagine with earthly thoughts. Yet they are as real as His promises. Today, don't be afraid to ask, for He waits to give—and that with good pleasure. And always hope with anticipation for the presently unseen gifts He has for you in eternity.

"You cannot need more than Christ has to give, is willing to
bestow, and will enrich you with in your every time of need."

ANNE DUTTON

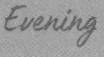

CITIZENSHIP

Now they desire a better country, that is, an heavenly:
wherefore God is not ashamed to be called their God:
for he hath prepared for them a city.

HEBREWS 11:16

The good news is not that someday we will be citizens of a new city. Our God—who has no shame in being called our God—has already prepared His heavenly city for us. Yes, we await our transfer there, but we are presently already citizens in that better country we desire. Whatever dreams we have tonight, they will pale in comparison to the reality of a city prepared for us by the Lord. Whatever images we have of that heavenly city are far too little, far too inadequate. After all, we're talking about a city prepared for us by *God*.

"Christianity removes the attraction of the earth;
and this is one way in which it diminishes men's
burden. It makes them citizens of another world."

HENRY DRUMMOND

OUR HOLY SWORD

*The word of God is quick, and powerful, and sharper than
any twoedged sword, piercing even to the dividing asunder
of soul and spirit, and of the joints and marrow, and is a
discerner of the thoughts and intents of the heart.*

HEBREWS 4:12

Among the many uses for God's Word is its role as a sword. With this lethal weapon we slay our spiritual enemies—but we also slay our inward enemies. Whatever remains in us of our old creation must be slain by the two-edged sword of God's Word.

Today you may encounter a part of you that needs to die because it is leading you in directions you don't want to go. Be quick about slaying the inner monster. Submit the neck of the enemy to the swift fall of the sword of God. Keep this sword unsheathed and sharpened until that final day.

*"The Word of God is a holy sword, which cuts asunder the lusts
of the heart! When pride begins to lift up itself, the sword of
the Spirit destroys this sin! When passion vents itself, the Word
of God, like Hercules' club, beats down this angry fury! When
lust boils, the Word of God cools that intemperate passion!"*

THOMAS WATSON

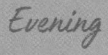

A RESTFUL NIGHT

Let my prayer be set forth before thee as incense;
and the lifting up of my hands as the evening sacrifice.

PSALM 141:2

The mighty sword of God is loosened against our enemies within and without by fervent prayer. Our prayers rise up as incense, our sword at the ready for battle. Just as we must be ruthless with ourselves, wielding the sword with passion, so must our prayers reinforce the work of the sword. We must be persistent in our petitions to God and relentless in our refusal to Satan's temptations.

Be diligent with the sword, slaying all enemies—but also be fervent in warfare prayer.

"Incense without fire makes no sweet smell. Prayer
without fervency is like incense without fire.... When
the heart is inflamed in prayer, a Christian is carried
as it were in a fiery chariot up to heaven."

THOMAS WATSON

MONITORING MY HEALTH

Pleasant words are as an honeycomb,
sweet to the soul, and health to the bones.

PROVERBS 16:24

Our faith is health to our emotional and spiritual well-being, but faith also can be health to our bodies. The apostle Paul considered our bodies as God's temples and thus we should take care of them. With today's proliferation of fast foods, junk foods, and genetically modified foods, we need to be all the more careful about the way we steward our temples.

Today, think twice before you jump on the sugar wagon. Take a good veggie break when you can. Eating living foods such as fruits and vegetables, as opposed to dead (often processed) foods, can do wonders toward bringing our temples up to code. A good way to thank God for our bodies is to treat them responsibly.

"Many things are pleasant that are not profitable, but these
pleasant words are health to the bones, to the inward man,
as well as sweet to the soul. They make the bones, which sin
has broken and put out of joint, to rejoice. The bones are the
strength of the body; and the good word of God is a means
of spiritual strength, curing the diseases that weaken us."

MATTHEW HENRY

GOD'S REST FOR THE WEARY

There remaineth therefore a rest to the people of God.

HEBREWS 4:9

Regarding our health and the stewardship of our bodies, we must be willing to eliminate the inner conflicts that negatively affect our well-being. Worry, anxiety, stress, and tension can rob us of the health we need to fulfill our calling. A good night's rest—without stress—is also conducive to good health.

God commanded the Israelites to celebrate a weekly Sabbath. He knew that the bodies He created would require rest—just as He, too, rested at the end of His work of creation.

Tonight, and every night, get the rest your body needs. This is a physical admonition, but a spiritual one too. A healthy, well-rested Christian will likely be more effective than a Christian who is worried, anxious, and tired.

"Resting in the Lord does not depend on external circumstances at all, but on your relationship to God Himself.... Deliberately tell God that you will not fret about that thing. All our fret and worry is caused by calculating without God."

OSWALD CHAMBERS

INTERCESSION
FOR FRIENDS

*Wherefore he is able also to save them to the
uttermost that come unto God by him, seeing he
ever liveth to make intercession for them.*

HEBREWS 7:25

Though different Christians have different callings, all Christians are called to prayer. Often those prayers are intercessions for friends in need. Becoming an intercessor for others is an easy task. Even a housebound person can pray for others. If you're praying for the needs of several people, it will help to have a prayer list at your side. Record the date you begin your intercession for a certain person and an end date when you've seen the results of your prayers.

Take this responsibility seriously. You will one day be on someone else's prayer list, if you are not already. And whenever you need the prayers of others, *ask!*

*"Jesus Christ carries on intercession for us in heaven; the
Holy Ghost carries on intercession in us on earth; and we
the saints have to carry on intercession for all men."*

OSWALD CHAMBERS

INTERCESSION FOR STRANGERS

I exhort therefore, that, first of all, supplications, prayers, intercessions, and giving of thanks, be made for all men.

1 TIMOTHY 2:1

We cannot pray regularly for others without feeling compassion for them. We're told by the apostle Paul to pray for all men. In so doing, it's fair to pay special attention to those we have deeper bonds with: members of our church fellowship, family, friends, and co-workers. But make sure to also pray for those with whom you may have differences.

Take time every day—perhaps in the evening—to intercede for others. In so doing, don't forget to pray for your enemies or those with whom you're in conflict. Prayer may bring about a resolution and healing to a broken relationship.

Intercede, too, for those in authority: the president, elected representatives, local first responders, and those over you in the workplace. Oh yes, and your pastor too!

"Earnest intercession will be sure to bring love with it. I do not believe you can hate a man for whom you habitually pray. If you dislike any brother Christian, pray for him doubly, not only for his sake, but for your own, that you may be cured of prejudice and saved from all unkind feeling."

CHARLES SPURGEON

ESTABLISHED IN THE FAITH

*As ye have therefore received Christ Jesus the Lord,
so walk ye in him: rooted and built up in him, and
stablished in the faith, as ye have been taught,
abounding therein with thanksgiving.*

COLOSSIANS 2:6-7

What do trials do for us? They put our trust to the test. We may ask, "Will God bring me through this trial?" The answer will always be yes. To be rooted, built up, and established in the faith means seeing our weak seedling tree of faith grow into a mighty oak of total trust. Do not despair during trials. God will see you through one more time—and every "one more time" after that.

*"As the same wind that blows down the poplar, only establishes
the oak; so the very storms which uproot the shallow professor
only establish the child of God more firmly in the faith of the
gospel. For though they may shake off some of his leaves, or
break off some of the rotten boughs at the end of the branch,
they do not uproot his faith, but rather strengthen it."*

J.C. PHILPOT

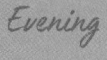

A FAITHFUL CALLING

*God is faithful, by whom ye were called unto
the fellowship of his Son Jesus Christ our Lord.*

1 CORINTHIANS 1:9

God has called us into fellowship—dare we say no to such a divine invitation? This fellowship with our Creator is the ultimate relationship. For His part, God offers us His strength for every necessary occasion. He knows only too well our own weakness. Thus in true faithfulness He stoops to supply us with power beyond ourselves, power that is always more than abundant to meet our need.

Don't despair over your weakness tonight. Instead, rejoice—our inability allows us to experience God's ability as we see the power of our Lord at work in our lives.

*"Our fellowship is with God, and fellowship is friendship, and
friendship means that partnership which, on His part, is
the accommodating of His strength to my weakness."*

G. CAMPBELL MORGAN

BEING A WITNESS

Ye shall receive power, after that the Holy Ghost is come upon you: and ye shall be witnesses unto me both in Jerusalem, and in all Judaea, and in Samaria, and unto the uttermost part of the earth.

ACTS 1:8

The Holy Spirit is given to all believers in Christ. And one important function of the Spirit is to enable us to be witnesses for Christ. He will supply words, when necessary, or He may so shine through our lives that others sense something different about us. Sadly, many believers may appreciate the Holy Spirit for the fruit He brings but are less interested in allowing Him to move through them as witnesses. Thus, many Christians miss divine appointments when they could easily and effectively share Christ with someone in need.

Be alert today. Perhaps the Holy Spirit wants to reach someone through your words or your life.

"The Church is the Body of Christ, and the Spirit is the Spirit of Christ. He fills the Body, directs its movements, controls its members, inspires its wisdom, supplies its strength. He guides into truth, sanctifies its agents, and empowers for witnessing. The Spirit has never abdicated His authority nor relegated His power."

SAMUEL CHADWICK

THE MAN WHO GIVES FREE BREAD TO THE HUNGRY

Watch thou in all things, endure afflictions, do the
work of an evangelist, make full proof of thy ministry.
2 TIMOTHY 4:5

Evangelism has been likened to introducing hungry people to a man who hands out free bread. We are all called to be witnesses for Christ—and without hesitation or fear. To be used in this way, we must open our eyes to the needs of others. Recall your own acceptance of Christ. Was it prompted by a need? Was it the result of a friend's witness? A pastor's powerful sermon? A book?

As you recount today's activities, can you recall opportunities when you might have shared your faith? Consider ending today with a prayer for tomorrow—that God will give you words that will influence others for Christ and that the Holy Spirit will use you in aid of others, whether it be in salvation or some other need.

"There is not a better evangelist in
the world than the Holy Spirit."
D.L. MOODY

A PURIFYING HOPE

*Beloved, now are we the sons of God, and it doth not
yet appear what we shall be: but we know that, when he
shall appear, we shall be like him; for we shall see him
as he is. And every man that hath this hope in him
purifieth himself, even as he is pure.*

1 JOHN 3:2-3

In this polluted world, we need all the means possible to become pure and stay pure. John teaches us that having the hope of Christ's return purifies us. A hope-filled, purified Christian stands out in today's world. To be pure is to escape the corruption of sensuality, degradation, and open evil in today's world. If we have not this purity, what good then is our so-called faith? Without purity, we are no different from the unsaved world. Today, bring to mind the purifying effect of seeing Christ as He is and becoming like Him. Because Christ is pure, we may be pure also.

*"A faith that does not work by love is spurious!
A hope that does not purify the heart is carnal!
A religion that does not make us holy is a delusion!"*

JAMES SMITH

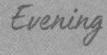
A LIVELY HOPE

*Blessed be the God and Father of our Lord
Jesus Christ, which according to his abundant mercy
hath begotten us again unto a lively hope by the
resurrection of Jesus Christ from the dead.*

1 Peter 1:3

Along with purity in the midst of today's polluted world, we must survive with a *lively* hope—not a deadly dread of the future. It is God's mercy that brings this kind of hope. It's not a casual expectancy, as if we "hope" it will rain today.

The lively hope God imparted to us sustains us as we go through life. The hope the world offers leaves us wanting.

Tonight, reflect on your lively hope. If your confidence is growing weak, ask God to renew your hope "according to His abundant mercy."

> *"As fast as any burdens are laid on you,
> cast them upon your God."*
>
> James Smith

FATIGUE

I can do all things through Christ
which strengtheneth me.

PHILIPPIANS 4:13

One common complaint among people today is fatigue. Often we're so busy we don't take time to rest, or we don't take good care of ourselves in other ways. We eat foods devoid of real nutrition, often bolting our meals down so we can get to the next item on our to-do list.

We are simply too busy.

There are three ways to battle fatigue—or prevent it if it's not presently a problem. First, take care of your body with the right foods and plenty of quality rest. Second, eliminate activities that take up energy but are time wasters. Third, trust God to provide the strength necessary for your daily duties. If you have much to do today, rely on the supernatural strength of Christ to enable you to do all that's necessary and to eliminate what is unnecessary.

"How is a Christian able to do duty, to resist temptation but
through Christ's strengthening?…Christ not only gives us
our crown but our shield. He not only gives us our garland
when we overcome but our strength whereby we overcome."

THOMAS WATSON

RENEWAL

They that wait upon the LORD shall renew their strength;
they shall mount up with wings as eagles; they shall run,
and not be weary; and they shall walk, and not faint.

ISAIAH 40:31

Now, at today's end, how was your day? Busy? It's good to be busy—as long as our busyness is productive. And being tired is good if the fatigue comes from necessary labor. In either case, the evening is a time for rest and renewal for tomorrow. If you're still busy in the evening, when will you find time to rest and renew?

Take time to affirm your surrender of human strength to His mighty divine strength. This affirmation can come by "waiting upon the Lord." Resting. Meditating on God's goodness and His gifts.

True surrender brings true strength.

"If we will only surrender ourselves utterly to the Lord, and will
trust Him perfectly, we shall find our souls 'mounting up with
wings as eagles' to the heavenly places in Christ Jesus, where
earthly annoyances or sorrows have no power to disturb us."

HANNAH WHITALL SMITH

MEDITATING

I remember the days of old; I meditate on all
thy works; I muse on the work of thy hands.

PSALM 143:5

When we pray, do we take God's presence for granted? Many of us are guilty of rushing through our prayers, asking God for this or that and then signing off with a quick "Amen." In so doing, we're missing out on a key element of prayer: quietly meditating on God and musing on the work of His hands. Wordless prayers are true prayers nonetheless. Today, sit quietly for a while in God's presence. Ask for nothing. Simply give thanks…and then consider the work of His hands.

"There come times when I have nothing more to tell God. If
I were to continue to pray in words, I would have to repeat
what I have already said. At such times it is wonderful to
say to God, 'May I be in Thy presence, Lord? I have nothing
more to say to Thee, but I do love to be in Thy presence.'"

OLE HALLESBY

GOD ON THE MIND

*My soul shall be satisfied as with marrow and fatness; and
my mouth shall praise thee with joyful lips: when I remember
thee upon my bed, and meditate on thee in the night watches.*

PSALM 63:5-6

Meditating on God in the "night watches" brings great peace to our souls. Our meditation will result in praise with joyful lips. Evening is a time to remember. Remember the presence of God as He accompanied you throughout the earlier hours of the day. Remember His work in bringing you to the place you're in now. Remember His promises meant for you. Remember that God has a perfect will for you.

Consider the future memories that the unfolding of God's will for you will bring.

Above all, remember His love for you. Delight yourself in Him. For it's when we're robbed of the joy of memory that we may be tempted to return to carnal pleasures.

*"No one can live without delight and that is why a man
deprived of spiritual joy goes over to carnal pleasure."*

THOMAS AQUINAS

RESPONSIBILITY

Every one of us shall give account of himself to God.
ROMANS 14:12

Who among us doesn't review our financial accounts to make sure the bills are all paid, our savings and investments in order, and our taxes current? So too should we take care that our spiritual life is in order. Have we neglected to deal with certain sins? Are our relationships with others free and clear? Is there an area of our life unsubmitted to God? A thorough spiritual inventory from time to time is good for all of us. If nothing more, it enables us to refresh our thanks to God for the debt we've owed that only Christ could pay.

Today is a good day to inquire of God, "Where am I lacking in my surrender to You?"

"Make up your spiritual accounts daily; see how matters stand
between God and your souls. Often reckonings keep God and
conscience friends. Do with your hearts as you do with your
watches, wind them up every morning by prayer, and at night
examine whether your hearts have gone true all that day, whether
the wheels of your affections have moved swiftly toward heaven."

THOMAS WATSON

A JOB WELL DONE

His lord said unto him, Well done, thou good and
faithful servant: thou hast been faithful over a few things,
I will make thee ruler over many things:
enter thou into the joy of thy lord.

MATTHEW 25:21

The final triumph for every believer is to hear the welcome words, "Well done, thou good and faithful servant." The resulting reward of entering into the joy of the Lord will be worth any seeming sacrifice made on earth. It is no small thing that we have a taste of eternal joy now, as we look forward to an eternity filled with joy— all because we've been good and faithful servants of God. Tonight, review your calling before God. Ask for greater vision for your life, for more ways to be that good and faithful servant. God will answer that prayer speedily.

"Oh, amazing! The saints enter into God's own
joy! They have not only the joy which God
bestows—but the joy which God enjoys!"

THOMAS WATSON

BRIDLING OUR TONGUE

If any man among you seem to be religious,
and bridleth not his tongue, but deceiveth
his own heart, this man's religion is vain.

JAMES 1:26

The words of James are sobering. Our profession of faith is in vain if our tongue betrays that faith. Our tongue only speaks what the heart tells it. Though we may blame the tongue, we must get at the root of our loose lips—the deceptive heart.

Today, let's consider our words. May the Holy Spirit nudge us when our tongue is about to speak unbridled words. When we deal with our wayward tongue, let us also consider what our eyes are allowed to see and where our feet are permitted to take us. May the Lord keep every part of our being safe from a deceptive heart.

"O Lord, keep our hearts, keep our eyes, keep
our feet, and keep our tongues."

WILLIAM TIPTAFT

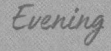

SAYING TRUTH

The lip of truth shall be established for ever:
but a lying tongue is but for a moment.

PROVERBS 12:19

It's not enough that we deal with the loose words of our unbridled tongue. We must also put our tongue to good use, speaking the truth in all cases. May the Lord help us to speak *good* words, not evil. May we utter blessings, not curses. May we build up with our tongues, not tear down. May we affirm others, not shame them. May we speak healing, not hurt.

O Lord, take our surrendered tongue tonight and train it to speak only your truth—established forever. Purify our tongues, Lord!

"The tongues of believers are bridled by a heartfelt
regard to truth, love and purity."

JOHN NEWTON

A WEDDING FEAST

*Blessed are they which are called unto
the marriage supper of the Lamb.*

REVELATION 19:9

What an event it will be! The marriage supper of the Lamb—a feast to which all are invited, though not all come. To be called to the greatest event of all time—and beyond time—is not to be missed!

Lord, make us ready today for that great banquet. Washed in the blood of the Lamb being honored, clothed in His righteousness, renewed by Your Spirit, meeting You in boldness and yet humility. Unworthy yet made worthy by the cross of Christ.

O Lord, come for Your people soon!

*"True Christians shall alone be found ready at the second
advent. Washed in the blood of atonement, clothed in Christ's
righteousness, renewed by the Spirit, they shall meet their Lord
with boldness, and sit down at the marriage supper of the
Lamb, to go out no more. Surely this is a blessed prospect."*

J.C. RYLE

An Everlasting Marriage

*Let us be glad and rejoice, and give honor to him:
for the marriage of the Lamb is come, and
his wife hath made herself ready.*

Revelation 19:7

Tonight we meditate on that coming great supper, prepared for all who have the kingdom of God in their hearts.

Lord, may the numbers of those seated at the table increase as the time draws near. Bring those inheritors of salvation to your family, Father. Prepare even now that blessed table where we shall dine with our King. May the coming feast honor the Lamb slain for us. May we be a fit bride for the groom whom we love. Fill us, O Lord, with great anticipation for the marriage of the Lamb.

*"If we are to sit down among those blessed ones who are
called unto the marriage supper of the Lamb…we must
have had 'the kingdom of God, which is righteousness and
peace and joy in the Holy Spirit' set up in our hearts."*

J.C. Philpot

PRAISE BREAKS

I will be glad and rejoice in thee:
I will sing praise to thy name, O thou most High.

PSALM 9:2

How often we neglect praise as part of our prayer time. Not just mouthing words of praise—as good as that is—but entering into a short season of praise alone, asking God for nothing but His presence.

Praise changes things—starting with us but not ending there. Praise is heard and appreciated by God. We must not let a day go by without a few "praise breaks" scattered throughout our hours. Get alone with God. Speaks words of honor, praise, and glory to the King of kings. Let your praise turn to worship. You will invigorate the rest of your day as you gain strength through the power of praise.

"Eternity will be too short fully to recount His praise. Let
us not shorten our joy by neglecting to begin on earth."

HENRY LAW

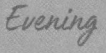

PRAISE ON OUR LIPS

*By him therefore let us offer the sacrifice
of praise to God continually, that is, the fruit
of our lips giving thanks to his name.*

HEBREWS 13:15

The writer of Hebrews was right to include the word *continually* in his call to offer the sacrifice of praise. The heart that is constantly attuned to the praise of God will be a joyful heart and a continual feast.

What has happened today for which you can offer praise? What do you look forward to tomorrow as an opportunity to praise God? The writer also adds this clarification to his call to praise: The fruit of our lips should give thanks to His name. Yes, praise and thanksgiving go together. If you begin to praise God, you will quickly turn to thanking Him. If you begin to thank Him, you will soon be praising Him. Either way, joy is the result!

> *"A thankful and a contented spirit is a continual feast. We
> ought to be contented, and we shall be contented, if we are
> in the habit of seeing God in everything, and living upon
> Him day by day. Oh, for a spirit of true thankfulness!"*
>
> ASHTON OXENDEN

A HAPPY LIFE

Whoso trusteth in the LORD, happy is he.
PROVERBS 16:20

Though sadness and tragedy are a part of every life, they are simply momentary clouds that hide the still-shining sun. When the clouds pass—as they always do—the brightness of the sun is once again apparent. The happy Christian knows this and bears up under fleeting adversity. Trusting in God throughout our daily trials is the path to happiness. The knowledge that His presence is always with us sustains us as we go through life, taking one step at a time. Every step toward Him is a step away from pain and a step toward happiness.

"God is such an infinite blessing that every sense of His glorious presence gives gladness to the heart. Every step toward Him is likewise a measure of happiness."
SUSANNA WESLEY

HAPPINESS IS A
DECISION FOR THE LORD

Happy is that people, whose God is the LORD.

PSALM 144:15

Anyone, including unbelievers, can experience some measure of happiness—often as events are going their way. But it is the Christian for whom happiness is a way of life. Why so? Because our God is the Lord, as the psalmist notes. We experience a joy that emanates not from earth but from heaven. This is a happiness that cannot be known by an unbelieving heart.

Would we be happy in life? Would we be happy tonight? We have but one route to that divine happiness—and that is through Christ. In Him we find a happiness exported from heaven to our hearts. But we must decide to have this happiness, just as one must receive an offered gift before it becomes theirs. Tonight, receive His happiness. Wake up tomorrow recalling your decision.

> *"There is a joy which is not given to the ungodly, but to those who love Thee for Thine own sake, whose joy Thou Thyself art. And this is the happy life, to rejoice to Thee, of Thee, for Thee; this it is, and there is no other."*
>
> AUGUSTINE

OUR IDENTITY

*Ye are a chosen generation, a royal priesthood, an
holy nation, a peculiar people; that ye should
show forth the praises of him who hath called
you out of darkness into his marvelous light.*

1 PETER 2:9

Every believer is part of a "chosen generation, a royal priesthood,
an holy nation, a peculiar people." The reason for our peculiar-
ity is that we should show forth the praises of God. We once walked
in darkness, but we were called out of darkness to walk in His "marvelous light."

Today, live as one who is distinct from the world, different in
every important aspect, always remembering we are not the ones
who made us distinct—God is. To Him alone belongs the glory.

*"The Lord's people are always represented as distinct from the
world and peculiarly set apart for the Lord. They are in the
midst of many people but are distinct from all people…. They
are viewed as a new creation, are claimed as Jehovah's first fruits,
and are commanded to imitate God as dear children. They
are to represent Jesus on earth, who represents them in Heaven;
and to be witnesses for God in their day and generation."*

JAMES SMITH

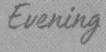
WHO I AM IN CHRIST

*If any man be in Christ, he is a new creature: old things
are passed away; behold, all things are become new.*
2 CORINTHIANS 5:17

We were born as human beings through a natural process. But when we were born again, it was through a supernatural process. The old "us" was set aside, passed away, reckoned dead so that the new creation would become our identity. Born of the Spirit, not of the flesh.

All of our post-conversion life is simply living out a new identity—that of a new creation, born from above by the Spirit of God. Believing it doesn't make it so. It already *is* so. Believing is simply our affirmation of what is true about ourselves.

Reckon yourself dead to sin and self and alive to righteousness.

> *"The Spiritual Life is the gift of the Living Spirit. The
> spiritual man is no mere development of the Natural
> man. He is a New Creation born from Above."*
> HENRY DRUMMOND

OUR FORGETFUL GOD

I, even I, am he that blotteth out thy transgressions
for mine own sake, and will not remember thy sins.

ISAIAH 43:25

Just how forgiven are we? Does God remember our sins, even as He's forgiven them? No! He has promised *not* to remember our sins, no matter how many, no matter how awful, no matter how recently or how long ago. Our sins are utterly *gone* from God's memory. Why then do we remember them? Why do we allow our accuser to whisper them in our ear?

True freedom recognizes the depth of God's forgiveness of our sins. We are fully saved, fully forgiven, fully empowered. We're not on probation, in fear of having our past sins paraded before us on Judgment Day.

Today, give thanks for God's willing forgetfulness.

"God ordains forgiveness absolute, unbounded, unrestricted,
unlimited, unfenced by boundaries, unconfined by barriers. He
erects a lofty throne, on which this grace supremely reigns."

HENRY LAW

A Short Memory

*I will be merciful to their unrighteousness, and their
sins and their iniquities will I remember no more.*

HEBREWS 8:12

What a joy it is to ponder God's way of dealing with our sins—
even the most heinous infractions. Though He forgets them,
that in no way means they were not paid for. Sin requires atonement. And God's way of accomplishing atonement was to provide
His innocent Son as a sin offering for our guilt. Sin wasn't just forgotten because of God's love for us. Sin was forgiven because the
price was paid. We can sleep well at night, knowing we have permanent peace with God.

> *"Though your sins are as many as the sands and as mighty
> as the mountains, I will drown them in the deeps of My
> bottomless mercies (Micah 7:19). I will be merciful to your
> unrighteousness. I will multiply your pardon (Hebrews 8:12;
> Isaiah 55:7); where your sins have abounded, My grace shall
> superabound; though they be as scarlet, they shall be white as
> snow; though red like crimson, they shall be as wool (Isaiah
> 1:18). Behold, I declare Myself satisfied and pronounce you
> absolved (Job 33:24). The price is paid, your debts are cleared,
> your bonds are canceled (Isaiah 43:25; Colossians 2:13-14)."*

JOSEPH ALLEINE

PRAYER FOR HEALTH

*Beloved, I wish above all things that thou mayest
prosper and be in health, even as thy soul prospereth.*

3 JOHN 1:2

God can use us best when we're healthy. Surely John had that in mind when he prayed for his readers to prosper both in their souls and in their bodily health. And like all that we receive from God, good health comes as a gift.

If illness strikes, never be reluctant to pray for healing and then to follow through as God leads, whether by medicine or miracle. Often, our healing can come by rejoicing and praising God in spite of our malady. So many illnesses are caused or made worse by stress, worry, and anxiety, all of which can be banished through praise… and trust.

Make health a priority as you pray today.

*"Begin to rejoice in the Lord, and your bones will
flourish like an herb, and your cheeks will glow with
the bloom of health and freshness. Worry, fear, distrust,
care—all are poisonous! Joy is balm and healing, and
if you will but rejoice, God will give power."*

A.B. SIMPSON

A RESTFUL, HEALTHFUL NIGHT

Be not wise in thine own eyes: fear the LORD,
and depart from evil. It shall be health to
thy navel, and marrow to thy bones.

PROVERBS 3:7-8

If you are in good health tonight, praise God and rest securely. If you are sick or in pain, praise God also and relinquish your health to Him. He is the Great Physician. No ailment is beyond His power to heal. In the Gospels we see that a very sick woman was healed when she barely touched the hem of His garment.

It's likely you know someone who is sick right now. Take a moment and pray for them. Thank God that He is the arbiter of their health. Ask Him to bring healing, and vow to give Him the glory for restoration.

"Health is good while the Lord preserves it and sickness is still
better when he appoints it. He is good when he grants our wishes
and multiplies our comforts—and he is good when he sends
us trials and crosses. We are short-sighted and cannot see how
many and what important consequences depend upon every
turn in life; but the whole chain of events are open to his view."

JOHN NEWTON

STRESS

Be careful for nothing; but in every thing
by prayer and supplication with thanksgiving
let your requests be made known unto God.

PHILIPPIANS 4:6

In our present and often troubling times, we tend to become stressed over matters large and small. And yet each such intrusion into our peace of mind can be remedied by God's directive to "be careful for nothing."

The proper response for stress is to bring every anxiety-filled situation before God in prayer, with thanksgiving. The Lord knows our stressors, and He hears our requests. Prayer is the great stress reducer, shifting the burden from our shoulders to God's mighty shoulders. Faith, as we pray, releases us from having to rely on merely human solutions and opens the door to God's perfect resolution.

"Resting in the Lord does not depend on external circumstances
at all, but on your relationship to God Himself.... Deliberately
tell God that you will not fret about that thing. All our
fret and worry is caused by calculating without God."

OSWALD CHAMBERS

DE-STRESS

Take therefore no thought for the morrow:
for the morrow shall take thought for the things of itself.
Sufficient unto the day is the evil thereof.

MATTHEW 6:34

Evening is a great time to review and relinquish any remaining worries and anxieties that interrupted our day. Even though we have prayed, we must also be sure we have left our stressful situation fully in God's hands. If you say the day has been a blessed day with no stresses, you must know that we live one day at a time, that there is no guarantee tomorrow will likewise be free of worries. Don't be anxious about future hardships and problems, but neither be complacent when your stress is minimal. You have grace for today, and you will also have grace for every tomorrow.

"The future with all its vicissitudes, is in His keeping and
ordering. You may work the loom—the shuttle may be in
your hands—but the pattern is all His—the intermingling
threads of varied hue, even what are dark and somber. Do
not talk of a tangled web, when it is that of the Great
Craftsman! Confide in that heart of Infinite Love!"

JOHN MACDUFF

WONDERS IN THE DEEP

*They that go down to the sea in ships, that do
business in great waters; these see the works
of the LORD, and his wonders in the deep.*

PSALM 107:23-24

"It's so safe to stay on shore. Let others sail out into the deep waters, not me." Ever think that way? What we don't realize is that God is out there on the ocean waters as well as on the safe shore.

At some point most of us have to make decisions about stepping out into potentially risky waters. If God is leading, we really must go, expecting His continued leading and His protective hands. If we say no to venturing into the deep, we may miss the miracles that can only happen out there. Venture out with confidence!

*"Let those who go to sea, consider and adore the Lord.
Mariners have their business upon the tempestuous ocean, and
there witness deliverances of which others cannot form an idea.
How seasonable it is at such a time to pray! …In answer to
their cries, the Lord turns their storm into a calm,
and causes their trials to end in gladness."*

MATTHEW HENRY

REFLECTING ON
GOD'S WONDERS

I will remember the works of the LORD:
surely I will remember thy wonders of old.

PSALM 77:11

The Christian life was not meant to be a dull life. God arranges many opportunities of sheer excitement for those brave enough to say yes to His will. For missionary Jim Elliot and his five co-laborers, his opportunity led to his death. But that was not the end of Jim's story. Later, his killers were reached for Christ. His widow, Elisabeth, went on to write several bestselling books that changed the lives of readers. It would take a real naysayer to say Jim's life was wasted. It's likely his death resulted in more fruit than had he lived.

Are you where God wants you? Are you willing to venture out for the Lord, even if it means your death? Though you most likely aren't called to be a missionary like Jim Elliot, you can be sure God's dream for you will be fruitful and ultimately exciting.

"Oh, the fullness, pleasure, sheer excitement
of knowing God on earth!"

JIM ELLIOT

CREATION

*Thou art worthy, O Lord, to receive glory and
honor and power: for thou hast created all things,
and for thy pleasure they are and were created.*

REVELATION 4:11

What if creation never existed? What if God never went to the trouble of creating the universe, the earth, human beings? He didn't have to. But He did. He created a world within a never-ending universe. He created a garden and set a man and woman in it. Then, thousands of years later, He created you. He created me. Again, He didn't have to. But in creating people, He fashioned souls with whom He could enjoy fellowship. He even went to the bother of creating prayer as a means of fellowship. Even more—as if more is necessary—He comes to live within us through His Holy Spirit.

Doesn't this make you incredulous? Isn't it all too wonderful? Who could imagine such a thing?

Today, bask in the majesty of creation. Today, enjoy fellowship with your Creator.

*"Happy the soul that has been
awed by a view of God's majesty."*

A.W. PINK

WE BEAR HIS IMAGE

So God created man in his own image,
in the image of God created he him.

GENESIS 1:27

As if creating our universe and fashioning us isn't enough, God made mankind in His own image. Every person bears the imprint of the Lord Himself. This is what makes the gift of life so important. Every baby is a reminder from God as to His identity.

Tonight, as you ready for bed, you may look in the mirror. Consider yourself as an image bearer of God. See in yourself the person God loves, the one whose fellowship He seeks out. You are that important to your Creator.

Meditate on such a miracle as you drift off to sleep.

"The heart is brought to love God by the love of God
being shed abroad in the heart; to love Jesus, by some sweet
manifestations of his mercy and grace; to love the people of
God, because they belong to Christ, and bear his image;
and to love the truth, because it makes them free."

J.C. PHILPOT

WAITING

Wait on the Lord: be of good courage,
and he shall strengthen thine heart:
wait, I say, on the Lord.

PSALM 27:14

Waiting on the Lord is a repeated admonition throughout the Bible—and deservedly so. We pray and expect a quick answer. But from God's point of view, the answer will come in His time, not ours. He is often the God of the eleventh hour, having given us the previous ten to trust Him.

There is another kind of waiting on the Lord too. That's when we just come into His presence and quietly wait before Him…like two old friends who simply enjoy one another's company. By either definition, waiting on the Lord is scriptural and part of His plan. As we wait, He will strengthen our heart. This morning, rather than ask for much, simply be still and wait on the Lord. Your unspoken prayers will be answered…in God's time.

"Never was a faithful prayer lost. Some prayers
have a longer voyage than others, but then they
return with their richer lading at last, so that the
praying soul is a gainer by waiting for an answer."

WILLIAM GURNALL

PATIENCE

If we hope for that we see not,
then do we with patience wait for it.

ROMANS 8:25

Have you ever prayed and not seen an answer? You are not alone. We often send up prayers only to realize that we must wait patiently for the answer. Yes, sometimes the answer comes immediately—but not often. Instead, God waits as we persist in prayer until He knows the time is right to supply the answer. Often, we see results only after we've given up the case as hopeless and recognized God as the only hope left.

Tonight, know that nothing you have prayed for is truly hopeless. *Hopeless* is not a word known to God, so let it also be unknown to us.

Be patient but persist in prayer. The God of hope will come through.

"It is in those times of hopeless chaos when the
sovereign hand of God is most likely to be seen."

THOMAS CHALMERS

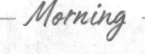

CRYING OUT TO GOD

The eyes of the LORD are upon the righteous,
and his ears are open unto their cry.

PSALM 34:15

There are prayers and then there are *prayers*! In desperation, we cry out to God for relief, for an answer, for deliverance—and are met with silence. But even in the seeming silence, God is speaking—and He is hearing. His ears are open to our cry, and He will come to our rescue precisely because of our need and His desire to meet it. The Lord does not view our requests with indifference. If we care about a matter, God also cares.

Is there a matter in your life that causes you to cry out to your Creator? Please know that He hears your cries, that the answer *will* come. And never forget that God is near, so very near, to those who cry out to Him.

"You need not cry very loud; he is nearer to us than we think."

BROTHER LAWRENCE

AN END TO OUR TEARS

God shall wipe away all tears from their eyes;
and there shall be no more death, neither sorrow,
nor crying, neither shall there be any more pain:
for the former things are passed away.

REVELATION 21:4

What have you cried out to God for today? Were there tears—if not literally, perhaps inner tears over a trial you're passing through? In reality, there are no tearless Christians. We all cry out to the Lord when meeting trials. In fact, our cries for relief are music to God's ears. They summon Him to action.

Know that God has heard your sobs today. He hears their echo yet again tonight. He has also seen your tears, and He looks to the day when He will wipe all tears from your eyes. In the meantime, He asks that our anguished cries include words of trust in His plan.

"Human friends can weep with us when we
weep. But Jesus is a friend, who, when He has
wept with us, can wipe away all our tears."

WILLIAM NEVINS

THE FAMILY OF GOD

*For this cause I bow my knees unto the Father of our
Lord Jesus Christ, of whom the whole family in heaven
and earth is named, that he would grant you, according
to the riches of his glory, to be strengthened with
might by his Spirit in the inner man.*

EPHESIANS 3:14-16

Every Christian is part of a family—God's family. Within this
family are all believers from the earliest chapters of Genesis,
down to the present day, with more to be added as the future unfolds.

Our present yearning is for that day when the entire family will
be united under the watchful eye of our heavenly Father. We shall
be sheltered under our Father's arms, nevermore to fear or worry.
Until then, His plan is to strengthen our inner man by the power of
His Holy Spirit. Even today, God is strengthening you. Keep your
eyes on the family connection as you long for that day of completion. The time is near.

*"Be of good cheer, Christian, the time is near when
God and you shall be as near as you can desire. You
shall dwell in His family! You shall then have joy
without sorrow and rest without weariness!"*

RICHARD BAXTER

NEVER ALONE!

*A father of the fatherless, and a judge of the widows,
is God in his holy habitation. God setteth the solitary in
families: he bringeth out those which are bound with
chains: but the rebellious dwell in a dry land.*

PSALM 68:5-6

A Christian need never feel alone. Not only is God with us, brooding over us in the night, but we have other believers worldwide who are part of God's family and who share our joy in Christ. We may not see them, but we can pray for them and thus draw close to them, even separated by continents. Every orphan, every widow, every lonely person has a home in Christ—and should have a home in our hearts, as we belong to the same forever family. God seeks out the lonely, and He sets the solitary in families.

"When the curtains of night close around you, He, to whom 'the darkness and the light are both alike,' is at your side! In the stillness of night, when in your wakeful moments, the visions of the departed flit before you like shadows on the wall, He, the sleepless Shepherd of Israel, is tending your couch, and whispering in your ear, 'Fear not, for I am with you!'"

JOHN MACDUFF

A SINGLE EYE

*The light of the body is the eye: if therefore thine
eye be single, thy whole body shall be full of light.*
MATTHEW 6:22

We would accomplish so much more for the Lord if we could simplify our goals with a single eye to accomplishing them. But unfortunately, more often than not, we're worn thin, scattered and stressed as we try to keep track of more projects than we can handle. We must occasionally ask, "What should I be doing that I'm not doing? And what can I eliminate from my life to make room for the needful things?"

It is the man or woman with the specific goal, and the single eye focused on that goal, that accomplishes much. Those who live scattered lives accomplish little.

Today, is your eye single? Is it focused clearly on God's destiny for you?

*"God, give me a deep humility, a well-guided
zeal, a burning love and a single eye!"*
GEORGE WHITEFIELD

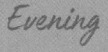

A FAITHFUL WORK

And another also said, Lord, I will follow thee; but let me
first go bid them farewell, which are at home at my house.
And Jesus said unto him, No man, having put his hand to
the plow, and looking back, is fit for the kingdom of God.

LUKE 9:61-62

The days, weeks, and months of our lives should be dominoes lined up in a row and falling against one another. In short, we need momentum. We need to be forward-thinking and forward-moving Christians. God has a work, a mission, for each of us. It may be small or large, but either way, it is *our* work and can be accomplished only when we move forward, not when we stand still or move in reverse. God will bring success, but only as we put our hands to the plow and keep looking ahead.

"Work! Walk through every open door; be ready in season and
out of season as if everything depended on your labor. This is
one of the great secrets in connection with successful service for
the Lord—work as if everything depended on your diligence,
and trust in the blessing of the Lord to bring success."

GEORGE MUELLER

THE SMALL THINGS

He that is faithful in that which is least
is faithful also in much: and he that is unjust
in the least is unjust also in much.

LUKE 16:10

Life is a proving ground of sorts. We are all given both large and small matters to contend with while we walk the earth. Some matters may be so small, we don't recognize them as assignments from God. Nevertheless, God *is* watching. He sees how we handle small tasks before He brings larger tasks our way. So too He measures our ability to judge justly by how just we are in small issues. If we're unjust, God takes note. If we're just, He may entrust more responsibility to us.

What small matters has He entrusted to you? Are there steps you need to take today to be faithful to that small matter in your keeping? Are you just in all dealings with others? God takes note.

"Wherever you are, be all there. Live to the hilt every
situation you believe to be the will of God."

JIM ELLIOT

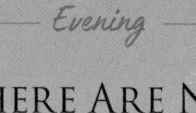
THERE ARE NO SMALL THINGS

Even the very hairs of your head
are all numbered. Fear not therefore:
ye are of more value than many sparrows.

LUKE 12:7

The God who counts the hairs of our head and values us more than many sparrows will not allow anything into our life that He will not be able to cast into a blessing for us if we but trust Him.

So deep is His love that there are no matters too small for His notice. Anything that concerns us also concerns God. We therefore have no need to fear any matter, small or large. As the old hymn tells us, "His eye is on the sparrow, and I know He watches me."

"He, who counts the very hairs of our heads and suffers not a
sparrow to fall without him, takes note of the minutest matters
that can affect the lives of his children, and regulates them all
according to his perfect will, let their origin be what they may."

HANNAH WHITALL SMITH

FULL ACCEPTANCE

To the praise of the glory of his grace,
wherein he hath made us accepted in the beloved.
EPHESIANS 1:6

If you were ever the last one chosen to be on the team, you know how important it is to feel valued and accepted, not merely tolerated. It's to the praise of His glory that on God's team, each of us is always the first one chosen.

No matter our past, we can have a better future when we know how loved and accepted we are by our Creator. If our past includes grievous sins or costly mistakes, God *still* elects us to be on the team. If our talents be small, the Lord accepts them and gives us assignments in accordance with our gifts.

Today, revel not only in God's love for you but also in His total acceptance of you…just as you are. On God's baseball team, we all get to be the pitcher.

"We serve a gracious Master who will overrule even our
mistakes to His glory and our own advantage."
JOHN NEWTON

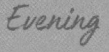
ACCEPTING OTHERS

*Receive ye one another, as Christ
also received us to the glory of God.*

ROMANS 15:7

One obvious lesson we learn from God's complete acceptance of us is that we too must accept others as they are, warts and all. It's like we're the team captain and are allowed to choose the players. Whom do we choose? Not the most athletic or the most generous. We choose each member of the team as our first pick. No one is left out. No one is not accepted. That's the power of Christ's acceptance of us. We must go and do likewise.

*"Our Lord has many weak children in His family, many
dull pupils in His school, many raw soldiers in His
army, many lame sheep in His flock. Yet He bears with
them all, and casts none away. Happy is that Christian
who has learned to do likewise with his brethren."*

J.C. RYLE

GOD'S ONLY CHILD—US!

For God so loved the world, that he gave his only
begotten Son, that whosoever believeth in him
should not perish, but have everlasting life.

JOHN 3:16

Think of it: Christ would have died for each of us—for you, for me—if we were the only ones needing redemption. God's love is so focused, it's as if each one of us is an only child, showered with all the benefits of the Lord's full attention, care, and love.

If anyone questions why God would allow someone to perish, they need only look at His sacrifice of Christ for the very reason that none should perish. His love is an individual love as well as a group love. Savor that knowledge today.

"He who counts the stars and calls them by their names,
is in no danger of forgetting His own redeemed children.
He knows your case as thoroughly as if you were the only
creature He ever made, or the only saint He ever loved!"

CHARLES SPURGEON

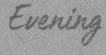

THE PERFECT FATHER

We have seen and do testify that the Father
sent the Son to be the Savior of the world.
1 JOHN 4:14

Christ's death on the cross was for each of us individually as well as corporately for all who would be saved. But it doesn't stop there. God's solitary care for us individually continues long after salvation—all through this mortal life and on into eternity. The Lord's love, like the universe, and like time itself, is endless. God is a Father forever, never changing, His love never waning, His eyes never averted from watching over us. He is the Savior of the world but also the Savior of each individual.

> *"He remembers our frame and knows that we are dust. He may sometimes chasten us, it is true, but even this He does with a smile, the proud, tender smile of a Father who is bursting with pleasure over an imperfect but promising son who is coming every day to look more and more like the One whose child he is."*
> A.W. TOZER

LOVING KINDNESS
IN THE MORNING

It is a good thing to give thanks unto the LORD,
and to sing praises unto thy name, O Most High:
to show forth thy lovingkindness in the morning…
PSALM 92:1-2

The best way to start every morning is to give thanks for another day and to sing praises to our Lord, showing forth His loving-kindness. But let's not let that be *just* the start of the day. Let the hours ahead also be filled with praise, even silent praise as we fulfill our daily duties. Being one who praises will not just change your day—it will change *you.*

And along with our praises, we can surely lift up our present needs. His loving-kindness listens for our petitions. Let us mix our praise with expectation, remembering that we cannot over-ask our heavenly Father for our needs.

"We cannot expect too little
from man nor too much from God!"
MATTHEW HENRY

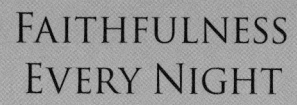

FAITHFULNESS
EVERY NIGHT

…and thy faithfulness every night.
Psalm 92:2

Faithful is our God at all times. For some, this faithfulness is best experienced at the close of day when we can look back over the hours and reflect on His goodness and constancy throughout the day. Unlike the busy daytime hours, evening is a time of slowing down and is conducive to reflection.

Be in no hurry tonight as you thank God for this day and once again leave any burdens on Him. Rest easy with anticipation for a new tomorrow and a fresh supply of His faithfulness.

"Gracious God! Look down upon me this night in Your great mercy. May I have now the inner sunshine of Your presence! Before I retire to rest, let me pitch my tent near Yourself, and enjoy the tokens of Your favor and blessing. Your loving-kindness has been new to me every morning, and Your faithfulness every night."
John MacDuff

GIVING THANKS
AS THE NEXT STEP

In every thing give thanks: for this is
the will of God in Christ Jesus concerning you.

1 THESSALONIANS 5:18

We don't always know the exact will of God—the next step to take. But one thing about the will of God we *do* know is that giving thanks *in all things* is never plan B. Perhaps it's when we're unsure of what to do, unsure of plan A, that giving thanks is most important.

Giving thanks in all things means in good times but also in adversity. We may need to repeatedly practice expressing gratitude to the Lord in all circumstances until it becomes a habit. Here are two very good reasons to adopt this habit: First, it's God's will, and second, gratitude can always be the next step when we don't know what to do.

Giving thanks can always be the perfect next step…in all things.

"If we would be happy we must train ourselves to be
grateful. Ingratitude makes life dreary for us."

J.R. MILLER

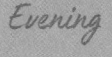

ALL THINGS

We know that all things work together
for good to them that love God, to them who
are the called according to his purpose.

ROMANS 8:28

During the deepest adversity, the harshest trials, the most depressing of events, we have one glorious promise from God to sustain us: No matter what happens, God is able to redeem the situation and weave it into a beautiful tapestry. That analogy comes from the old poem that tells us that looking at a tapestry from the back, we see no possible pattern, just a jumble of threads. To see what's really the work of art, we must turn the tapestry right side up and see how all those well-selected and carefully woven threads justify the ugly underside.

Trust in the promise of God tonight that He is weaving the threads of your life as only the Master Weaver can do.

"Well may we, in the worst that befalls us have a psalm
of thankfulness, because God works all things for our
good. Oh, be much in giving thanks to God!"

THOMAS WATSON

GOD'S WILL

I know the thoughts that I think toward you,
saith the LORD, thoughts of peace, and not
of evil, to give you an expected end.

JEREMIAH 29:11

Each of us has a veiled future. We don't know what tomorrow holds. And it's best this way. God has so designed it that we must live day by day, trusting Him. If we knew tomorrow held a fresh trouble, we might try to avoid it. But what if in that trouble lies God's blessing? We know that trials are given us to further the Lord's inner work in us. Can we therefore be content to just trust, instead of being curious about a future only God knows?

"It's better that we should not know our future. If we did, we
would often spoil God's plan for our life. If we could see
into tomorrow, and know the troubles it will bring, we
might be tempted to seek some way of avoiding them, while
really they are God's way to new honor and blessing…. It is
better, therefore, to walk with God, not knowing the path
ourselves, than it would be to see the way and choose for
ourselves. God's way for us—is always better than our own."

J.R. MILLER

DOING GOD'S WILL

The world passeth away, and the lust thereof:
but he that doeth the will of God abideth for ever.

1 JOHN 2:17

Are we concerned about doing God's will? We must remember that His will always trumps ours. His will prevails, though He chooses to let it prevail through us. Wonder of all wonders that God allows us to participate in the unfolding of His sovereign plan. We are all vessels, fit for use by our Master. Let us be ever mindful that His will *will* be done, but will we allow it to be done by *us*? May we not be slack in attending to His revealed will for us.

"I am no longer anxious about anything, as I realize the Lord is
able to carry out His will—and His will is mine. It makes no
matter where He places me, or how. That is rather for Him to
consider than for me; for in the easiest positions, He must give me
His grace; and in the most difficult, His grace is ever sufficient."

HUDSON TAYLOR

A MEASURED LIFE

So teach us to number our days,
that we may apply our hearts unto wisdom.

Psalm 90:12

The expression *killing time* is more accurate than we might realize. When we waste time, we are indeed killing it. It's not unlike throwing money out the car window as we speed down the freeway. For some Christians, it's necessary to budget time as well as money.

Time is a gift, a finite resource from God that we must steward carefully. Today, try to spot ways you may be killing time. Consider better uses of the hours, the minutes, the seconds you have. Your life, like all lives, is limited.

Time will eventually run out. Don't be so careless with the moments of your life that in your final days you'll regret the wasted hours.

"If you saw a man standing by the sea and flinging
diamonds into the water you would say he was insane.
Yet some of us are standing by the sea and flinging the
diamond days, one by one, into its dark floods!"

J.R. Miller

GOD DOES THE MEASURING

The days of our years are threescore years and ten;
and if by reason of strength they be fourscore years,
yet is their strength labor and sorrow; for
it is soon cut off, and we fly away.

PSALM 90:10

The hours given to us are like money in a piggy bank. We know there's money there—we just don't know how much or how little. So too with time: We have a limited number of days ahead of us, but we don't know how many or how few. Today, one more "dollar" of time was removed from the piggy bank. Tomorrow, another will fly away. Tend to this present moment with care; don't let it be wasted.

"Dispatch the work of your day and generation with speed
and diligence.... Whatever is incumbent upon you to do
for God's honor, and the good of others, either as the duty of
your station, or by special opportunity put into your hand,
perform it seasonably, if you would die comfortably."

THOMAS BOSTON

A SHELTER IN THE STORM

*Thou hast been a strength to the poor, a strength to
the needy in his distress, a refuge from the storm.*

ISAIAH 25:4

One advantage to storms is that they drive us into our shelter. Spiritual, relational, and circumstantial storms drive us into the refuge of our heavenly Father. When a storm approaches, don't run from the storm; run to the shelter of God's protection. He is, after all, a strength to us when we're in need.

The storm, unable to bring lasting damage, will soon leave. But the fruit gained by sheltering with God will last well into the sunshine days.

*"Did you never run for shelter in a storm, and find fruit which
you expected not? Did you never go to God for safeguard,
driven by outward storms, and there find unexpected fruit?"*

JOHN OWEN

EVERY STORM WILL CEASE

He maketh the storm a calm,
so that the waves thereof are still.

PSALM 107:29

Storms are temporary. God's peace is permanent. The blustery winds will soon cease, the rain will dry up, the clouds will move on. What remains after the storm is the calm that Christ brings. And take note that *He* maketh the storm a calm. During His earthly ministry, Jesus took authority over a literal storm, and our Father God can likewise calm the storms of life.

Our duty in a storm is to seek His shelter. It's not up to us to move the storm along—only God can do that.

"Let this encourage those of you who belong to Christ: the storm
may be tempestuous, but it is only temporary. The clouds that
are temporarily rolling over your head will pass, and then
you will have fair weather, an eternal sunshine of glory."
WILLIAM GURNALL

RANDOM ACTS OF KINDNESS

*Be ye kind one to another, tenderhearted, forgiving one
another, even as God for Christ's sake hath forgiven you.*

EPHESIANS 4:32

The gifts most fun to give are those that are unexpected or even anonymous. Surely we can all recall times when the Lord surprised us with a very welcome yet unexpected gift. Giving is God's nature, and it is also ours as His new creations.

Sometime today do something kind and unexpected for someone you know or even for a stranger. It can be as simple as an affirming phone call or a bouquet of flowers. It can be noticing a homeless person through eye contact and a respectful greeting.

Kindness has a way of rewarding those who practice it. What you sow, you will reap.

Show the love of God to one of His children today.

*"The greatest thing a man can do for his Heavenly
Father is to be kind to some of His other children."*

HENRY DRUMMOND

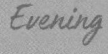

DIVINE ACTS OF KINDNESS

*That in the ages to come he might show the exceeding riches
of his grace in his kindness toward us through Christ Jesus.*

EPHESIANS 2:7

Our example of kindness comes directly from God, who routinely visits His people with unexpected blessings, every one of which serves as a reminder of His love for us and compels us to be a tangible blessing to others.

Who has God used lately to bless you? Behind that kindness was the hand of God reaching out to you through the effort of another. Don't break the chain of kindness. Reach out to others with the hand of Christ—*your* hand.

Tonight, call up from memory some past kindnesses God worked through the hands of another, and thank Him again.

*"Seek to cultivate a buoyant, joyous sense of the
crowded kindnesses of God in your daily life."*

ALEXANDER MACLAREN

LEAVING THE
CHOICE TO GOD

*Trust in the Lord with all thine heart; and
lean not unto thine own understanding. In all thy ways
acknowledge him, and he shall direct thy paths.*

Proverbs 3:5-6

The path of life we imagine for ourselves will almost certainly differ from God's far better plan. The secret to knowing this plan and benefiting from it is that we must want God's will strongly enough to trust Him with all our heart, so much so that we don't lean to our own understanding. As we acknowledge Him in all our ways, we won't have to try and guess the Lord's path for us. The true path—the one of God's choosing, the one that leads to our happiness—will become apparent.

*"Nothing can overturn the mind which abides in faith.
Nothing can destroy me which does not first unsettle
and destroy my faith. While I continue to believe, I
am secure against every danger. Faith in God meets
every charge and every foe with perfect success."*

Stephen Tyng

ACCEPTING GOD'S
CHOICE FOR MY LIFE

*Mary said, Behold the handmaid of the Lord; be it unto me
according to thy word. And the angel departed from her.*

LUKE 1:38

Ready acceptance of God's plan for our surrendered life will produce more fruit and make us more productive instruments in God's hands than our own paltry plans ever could. Our Creator sees what we cannot see. He has orchestrated a life for us that is a divine destiny.

Yes, God's grand plan includes us personally and all that befalls us. Without our existence, His plan would be incomplete. God didn't create us as mere placeholders in history but as participants of His choosing. It is no small thing to ponder that the Lord's eternal plan must include us.

Mary accepted God's plan though it can't have been an easy assignment. Her reward has been the admiration of surrendered Christians who, like her, will say to God, "Be it unto me according to thy word."

*"Let God have your life;
He can do more with it than you can."*

D.L. MOODY

THE BLOOD OF CHRIST—
OUR ATONEMENT

In whom we have redemption through his blood, the
forgiveness of sins, according to the riches of his grace.

EPHESIANS 1:7

The gospel isn't just about a man dying for sinners to give us eternal life. That's certainly a key element, but at the heart of the gospel is the shed blood of Christ. Without the blood, there is no remission of sins. Without the remission of sins, there is no gospel. Our celebration of the Lord's Supper is a celebration of the body and the blood. A bloodless Christianity is no Christianity at all—just another vain philosophy or ineffectual "religion" putting forth other illegitimate means of friendship with God.

Today, do not shrink back at the thought of the blood of Christ. Embrace the mystery and be thankful.

"When He separates any one to Himself,
He plants the blood of Christ right behind them."

G.V. WIGRAM

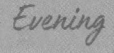
ONE DIED FOR ALL

*The love of Christ constraineth us; because we
thus judge, that if one died for all, then were all
dead: and that he died for all, that they which live
should not henceforth live unto themselves, but
unto him which died for them, and rose again.*

2 CORINTHIANS 5:14-15

Though the gospel is God's free gift of salvation, there was a price
paid for it. Not by us but by Christ. The love of God for sinners
was made manifest by the shed blood and broken body of Jesus. The
fact is, we cannot atone for our own sins; we need a Savior—and in
Christ we have that Savior. From his death and resurrection comes
all the peace that we need to make it through life's journey.

*"Christians are to labor in Christ's vineyard; and to show
forth his praises…. They have talents to consecrate to his
service, and they are to be fruitful in every good word and
work. But none can be so without Christ, who is our life. He
dwells in us as the sun lives in the garden, by his influence
producing fragrance and fruits; or as the soul lives in the
body actuating every limb, and penetrating every particle."*

WILLIAM NICHOLSON

FULLY INVESTED

Lay up for yourselves treasures in heaven,
where neither moth nor rust doth corrupt, and
where thieves do not break through nor steal.
MATTHEW 6:20

We make earthly investments in hopes of financial gain. But how are our heavenly investments? Jesus advises us to lay up treasures for ourselves not on earth but in heaven. Earthly investments can fail—and often do. But heavenly investments are fully ensured by the Word of God. Set aside your concerns about your earthly portfolio. Consider today ways to increase the moth- and rust-proof investments that last forever.

"Do not seek large estates, nor regard your worldly possessions
as your chief good; but seek first and most earnestly the
kingdom of God and the righteousness thereof. Secure
for yourselves the happiness of Heaven and consider
God, and the light of His countenance, and the graces
of His Spirit as your most valuable treasure. Make
them the supreme object of your desire and pursuit."
EDWARD GRIFFIN

YOU CAN TAKE IT WITH YOU

*Sell that ye have, and give alms; provide yourselves bags
which wax not old, a treasure in the heavens that faileth not,
where no thief approacheth, neither moth corrupteth.*

LUKE 12:33

There's an old saying: "You can't take it with you." True, we can't take earthly goods with us. Those material riches of this life end at the grave. But there *are* riches we can take with us, even send on ahead. Those riches are the investments we make in God's kingdom. These investments are comprised of our trust in God, the completion of our earthly assignment, and remembering the poor, hurt, and broken. When we have helped others, we have helped Christ. We may die poor in this life but wake up in heaven rich indeed—all because we made the wisest investment while on earth.

*"There is a way of using money, which makes it a curse. But
there is a way of using money, which makes it a blessing…. We
can…bank our possessions in Heaven, as we go through this
world, send our money on in advance, so that when we reach
there we shall find all our treasures laid up waiting for us."*

J.R. MILLER

DAILY PROVISION

Give us this day our daily bread.

MATTHEW 6:11

God gives us our daily bread with an emphasis on *daily*. Why is this? Because He wants us to trust Him for *today's* needs. When tomorrow becomes today, our needs will be supplied again.

As it is with bread, so too is it with grace and mercy. We are each given a daily supply. True, God's grace and mercy never run out, and thus they will be present for tomorrow's needs as well. But as with bread, God wants us to rely on Him for a fresh supply of all our needs *daily*. Can you give thanks for today's supply of bread—and of grace and mercy?

"Beloved Christian reader, in matters of grace you need a daily supply. You have no store of grace. Day by day you must seek help from above. It is a very sweet assurance that a daily portion is provided for you. In the Word, through the ministry, by meditation, in prayer, and waiting upon God—you shall receive renewed strength. In Jesus, all needful things are laid up for you. Then enjoy your continual allowance! Never go hungry while the daily bread of grace is on the table of mercy!"

CHARLES SPURGEON

ENOUGH FOR ONE DAY

I am the living bread which came down from heaven:
if any man eat of this bread, he shall live for ever:
and the bread that I will give is my flesh, which
I will give for the life of the world.

JOHN 6:51

God gives us our daily bread to replenish our bodies. He also gives us Christ as the bread from heaven, that we may "eat thereof and not die" (John 6:50). Today you ate the bread of good food supplied by God. Now, have you also feasted on heaven's bread in the person of Christ? Evening is the perfect time to give thanks and to partake of Christ to replenish our souls.

"When the devil sees a person discontented with daily bread,
he says, 'Here is good fishing for me!' Satan often tempts
discontented ones to murmuring, and to unlawful means,
cozening and defrauding; and he who increases an estate by
indirect means, stuffs his pillow with thorns so that his head
will lie very uneasy when he comes to die. If you would be freed
from the temptations which discontent exposes to, be content
with such things as you have—thank God for 'daily bread.'"

THOMAS WATSON

A LIFE PLEASING
TO THE LORD

Beloved, if our heart condemn us not, then have we
confidence toward God. And whatsoever we ask, we
receive of him, because we keep his commandments,
and do those things that are pleasing in his sight. And
this is his commandment, That we should believe
on the name of his Son Jesus Christ, and love
one another, as he gave us commandment.

1 JOHN 3:21-23

How do we please God? In the same way we approach any other aspect of the Christian life—by faith. Throughout His earthly walk, we see Christ time and again praise those who approached Him with faith. And He often chided those who would not believe.

Doing the things that are pleasing to God is a matter of obedience. If we know what to do and refuse to do it, that displeases the Lord. Doing the known will of God brings blessing and the sure knowledge that we please our heavenly Father. Never delay in doing what must be done. Delayed obedience is disobedience.

"Whether we think of, or speak to, God, whether we act
or suffer for him, all is prayer, when we have no other
object than his love, and the desire of pleasing him."

JOHN WESLEY

FRUITFUL IN EVERY GOOD WORK

*That ye might walk worthy of the Lord unto
all pleasing, being fruitful in every good work,
and increasing in the knowledge of God.*

COLOSSIANS 1:10

Whether we are young or old, looking forward to a lifetime of doing God's will or looking back at the years in which we obeyed His known will, we can turn to Christ and see how He has been with us through every good work assigned to us.

As long as our earthly life continues, we have daily opportunities to please Him, to be fruitful in every good work. And when we choose to collaborate with the Creator in every good work He puts before us, we increase in our knowledge of God. It then becomes clear that our assignments have the goal of blessing *us* by a deeper walk with our Lord.

*"There is only one way to be revived and healed from our
backslidings so that we may become fruitful even in old age.
We must take a steady look at the glory of Christ in His special
character, in His grace and work, as shown to us in the Scripture."*

JOHN OWEN

GODLINESS AND HOLINESS

The day of the Lord will come as a thief in the night;
in the which the heavens shall pass away with a great noise,
and the elements shall melt with fervent heat, the earth
also and the works that are therein shall be burned up.
Seeing then that all these things shall be dissolved,
what manner of persons ought ye to be in
all holy conversation and godliness?

2 PETER 3:10-11

Sometimes it seems that words like *holiness* and *godliness* have become absent from our vocabulary. The concepts sound stuffy, old-fashioned, even legalistic. But from God's point of view, godliness and holiness are as modern now as they ever were. The idea of an unholy Christian is an oxymoron. Holiness is required of believers, but true holiness—the *only* kind of holiness—isn't the putting on of a dour religious mask. Our holiness is an imputed holiness that we receive by faith and live out in our daily life. You may be tempted today by unholy desires. Resist them and put on the holiness of Christ by faith.

"May God so fill us today with the heart of Christ that
we may glow with the divine fire of holy desire."

A.B. SIMPSON

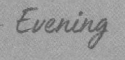

WHOLLY HOLY

You, that were sometime alienated and enemies in
your mind by wicked works, yet now hath he reconciled in
the body of his flesh through death, to present you holy
and unblameable and unreproveable in his sight.

COLOSSIANS 1:21-22

How holy is the believer? *Fully* holy. *Wholly* holy. How so? Because our holiness is the holiness of Christ. We dare not approach the Lord with our own brand of holiness. Such fakery would burn up at His very gaze. The only holiness God recognizes is the holiness of His Son, imputed to us. If you've been wearing a religious mask that feigns holiness, tonight is the perfect opportunity to remove the mask and put on the holiness of Christ.

"We have only to behold the Lamb of God who takes away
the sin of the world, and believe that He has borne our
griefs and carried our sorrows, and will soon present
us spotless and unblameable in His Father's sight."

J.C. RYLE

THE HIDDEN LIFE

In the time of trouble he shall hide me in his pavilion:
in the secret of his tabernacle shall he hide me;
he shall set me up upon a rock.

PSALM 27:5

It's not about us. It's about Him. It has always been about Him.

A good inventory of our motives is always in order. Are we here to be served or to serve? Are we content with God's way of using us…or do we envy the gifts of others?

There is something freeing about letting go of one's human expectations of being used by God in some flashy manner. There is power in the hidden life—the life of prayer behind closed doors, the praying of others into the kingdom, the financial support we give to those on the front lines of God's work. It is a great thing to be cut loose from high (and false) expectations.

"Exalt Christ. Use a sharp knife with yourself. Say little,
serve all, pass on. This is true greatness, to serve unnoticed
and work unseen. Oh, the joy of having nothing and
being nothing, seeing but a living Christ in glory, and
being careful for nothing but His interests down here."

JOHN NELSON DARBY

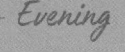

THE UNHIDDEN LIFE

That ye may be blameless and harmless, the sons of God,
without rebuke, in the midst of a crooked and perverse
nation, among whom ye shine as lights in the world.

PHILIPPIANS 2:15

Just as there is a time for the hidden Christian life on our knees in our prayer closet, so too is there a time for the unhidden Christian life where we shine as lights in the midst of a crooked and perverse nation.

The unhidden Christian life happens when we rise up from our knees, venture out of our prayer closet, and put shoe leather to our prayers. In your memory, has there ever been a more pressing need for Christians ablaze with God and ready to speak forth His truth?

May we each learn when to live the hidden life on our knees and when to live the unhidden, even bold, life in this darkening world.

"To be good at all times is a Christian's duty, but to
be good in bad times is a Christian's glory."

MATTHEW MEAD

TRUE PEACE

The peace of God, which passeth all understanding,
shall keep your hearts and minds through Christ Jesus.

PHILIPPIANS 4:7

Today is a day to enjoy the peace of God—the peace that surpasses all understanding. Circumstances may threaten our peace. Other people may try to intrude on our peace. Small irritations may accumulate and attempt to rob us of our peace. But we are not subject to these and other potential disruptions, because our peace comes from God—not from man, not from our personality, and certainly not from our circumstances. Our peace comes as a result of our trust in a trustworthy Creator. We cannot be rattled when governed by the peace of our Lord.

"Christian peace is the calm of the heart which is
not dependent on any external circumstances and
which no circumstances, however full of danger or
alarm, can break. Its secret is perfect trust in God."

J.R. MILLER

LIVE IN PEACE

Be perfect, be of good comfort, be of one mind, live in peace;
and the God of love and peace shall be with you.

2 CORINTHIANS 13:11

Knowing the peace of God will lead us into knowing the will of God. In fact, peace is always a hallmark of God's will, even when His will is fraught with danger or trials.

Hurry robs us of peace. With this in mind, we must slow down and refuse the hurriedness that disrupts our serenity of heart.

Tonight, be at peace. Know that God will speak to you in stillness, not in noise. Seek His will in all you do. Stay focused on the Lord, confident in the knowledge that He is focused on you.

"Blessed are the single-hearted, for they shall enjoy much peace....
If you refuse to be hurried and pressed, if you stay your soul on
God, nothing can keep you from that clearness of spirit which
is life and peace. In that stillness you know what His will is."

AMY CARMICHAEL

A PROSPEROUS FUTURE

*Blessed is the man that walketh not in the counsel of the
ungodly, nor standeth in the way of sinners, nor sitteth in the
seat of the scornful. But his delight is in the law of the LORD;
and in his law doth he meditate day and night. And he
shall be like a tree planted by the rivers of water, that
bringeth forth his fruit in his season; his leaf also shall
not wither; and whatsoever he doeth shall prosper.*

PSALM 1:1-3

Face it, God wants us to succeed, to be prosperous even—not
necessarily financially prosperous, but prosperous in what we're
called to do and who we're called to be. God doesn't call us to failure.

This blessing, though, is reserved for those who don't walk the
way of the ungodly. Only those who delight in the law of the Lord
can expect God's blessing, can confidently anticipate that whatsoever they do, they shall indeed prosper.

Today, are you walking in the way of prosperity?

*"When a man becomes a Christian, he becomes industrious,
trustworthy and prosperous. Now, if that man when he gets
all he can and saves all he can, does not give all he can, I
have more hope for Judas Iscariot than for that man!"*

JOHN WESLEY

FORGETTING THE PAST

Brethren, I count not myself to have apprehended:
but this one thing I do, forgetting those things which
are behind, and reaching forth unto those things
which are before, I press toward the mark for the
prize of the high calling of God in Christ Jesus.

PHILIPPIANS 3:13-14

God has called us not to a past but to a future. The past is dead. It can't be resurrected. All we have is a future—and how we act now, the decisions we make now will determine what kind of future we will have.

One aspect of living that good future is having the ability to forget certain events in our past. We can't reach our hand out to grasp the future while still maintaining a grip on the past. Tonight, consider past events that may be hindering you from "reaching forth unto those things which are before." Let go of those, and reach out confidently for the prize of the high calling of God in Christ Jesus.

> *"We can only effectually serve Christ as we are enjoying*
> *Him…. The man who will present Christ to others*
> *must be occupied with Christ for himself."*
> C.H. MACKINTOSH

REIGNING IN LIFE

If by one man's offence death reigned by one; much more
they which receive abundance of grace and of the gift of
righteousness shall reign in life by one, Jesus Christ.

ROMANS 5:17

D o you ever feel under the pile? Like you're being controlled by events, rather than controlling them? That's not the way God wants us to live. His desire is that we "reign in life" by Jesus Christ. He has paid it all. He has taken our sins and our burdens. And as long as we follow Him, we will reign. But if we stray by taking on matters that are not His will for us, we may find ourselves under the pile again.

Today, get out from under the pile. *Reign.*

"If the will of God is our will, and if He always has His
way, then we always have our way also, and we reign in a
perpetual kingdom. He who sides with God cannot fail to
win in every encounter; and, whether the result shall be joy
or sorrow, failure or success, death or life, we may, under all
circumstances, join in the Apostle's shout of victory, 'Thanks be
unto God which always causeth us to triumph in Christ!'"

HANNAH WHITALL SMITH

SEATED ABOVE

*Even when we were dead in sins, hath quickened us
together with Christ, (by grace ye are saved;) and hath
raised us up together, and made us sit together
in heavenly places in Christ Jesus.*

EPHESIANS 2:5-6

Our position as lost men and women mandated that our eyes should be focused on this earthly life. But when we came to Christ, many changes took place. One such change was our position. We were removed from an earthly position and made to sit together with Christ in heavenly places. It's from this new position that we reign in life. We're no longer subject to the aftermath of earthly calamities in life. They may still occur, but we are now different, by virtue of our heavenly position and new creation.

*"It is His pure grace, and a grace that has saved us, that
found us dead in sins, and brought us out of death even as
Christ came out of it, and by the same power, and brought
us out with Him by the power of life in resurrection with
Christ, to set us in the light and in the favor of God, as
a new creation, even as Christ Himself is there."*

JOHN NELSON DARBY

WORSHIP

God is a Spirit: and they that worship him
must worship him in spirit and in truth.

JOHN 4:24

Not all so-called worship is true worship. In fact, though the religions of the world have many varieties of worship, all attempts at worship fail if they don't emanate from the spirit, if they're not based on truth.

Worship must not just be the fruit of our lips, but it must arise from a deeper place within us. For us, the redeemed, we know from whence we came. We know how lost we were. That realization causes thanksgiving, praise, and yes, worship to rise up within us in eternal gratitude. This God we worship—this Savior—is the sole occupation of our own deep-within spirit. True worship comes from knowing the full deliverance we've received through Christ and thus exalting Him.

"True worship is the adoration of a redeemed
people, occupied with God Himself."

A.W. PINK

QUIET PRAISE

Be still, and know that I am God:
I will be exalted among the heathen,
I will be exalted in the earth.

PSALM 46:10

There are admonitions in the Old Testament about shouting our praises to God, so that is certainly a valid way to glorify our Creator. But so is silent praise. Just as God hears the loud cries of praise, He also hears the whispers and silent words of adoration.

Tonight, end your day knowing that God is always at work in you. Offer up silent words of praise. Perhaps even enjoy a few minutes of utter stillness, savoring His presence just as He savors yours.

"Be still for God is working. He is the great Agent, whoever
and whatever may be the instruments. He leaves nothing to
chance. There is no contingency with him. He works according
to a settled plan, and with a fixed end in view. While God
is working you are to be still, you are to be silent; it will
end better than you expect, as well as you could wish."

JAMES SMITH

BOUNDARIES

*Be ye not unequally yoked together with unbelievers: for
what fellowship hath righteousness with unrighteousness?
and what communion hath light with darkness?*

2 CORINTHIANS 6:14

Would you drive confidently on a narrow road winding around a cliff if there were no guardrails? At a minimum, it would be dangerous. At the maximum, it could be fatal. In a similar way, when we Christians live without boundaries, we're courting spiritual danger. Because of the grace God extends to us, we may overlook the boundaries that keep us safe. For instance, we live in a sexually brazen culture. For Christians who have no boundaries regarding their sexual lives, there are dangers that could affect their ability to enjoy fellowship with God, not to mention the risk of sexually transmitted diseases. Each of us must be aware of which areas of our life need guardrails to keep us safe. Take time today to evaluate your weaknesses and ask yourself if you need to implement boundaries.

Don't look to the world for your boundaries. You won't find them there.

*"One of the greatest evils, at the present day, with which
the Church has to contend, is conformity to the world."*

WILLIAM NICHOLSON

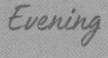

WISE COUNSEL

By wise counsel thou shalt make thy war:
and in multitude of counsellors there is safety.

PROVERBS 24:6

When we consider the necessary guardrails and boundaries we need to implement, we must keep in mind the wise counsel of our mature brothers and sisters in Christ. Some men prudently belong to a small accountability group where sharing is kept confidential and prayer power is abundant.

Another helpful guardrail consists of simply avoiding triggers that may lead to the violation of a boundary. You may need to set boundaries with certain places, music, movies, and even friends if particular relationships cause you to compromise.

Remember, as a Christian, you're in a war. You can't win the war alone. Seek out wise counselors, some of whom can help you set up the needed guardrails. The road along the cliffs is indeed dangerous.

"A multitude of wise counselors are far more useful to a nation
engaged in war, than a great number of valiant soldiers."

GEORGE LAWSON

PARTAKERS OF
THE DIVINE NATURE

*Whereby are given unto us exceeding great and
precious promises: that by these ye might be partakers
of the divine nature, having escaped the corruption
that is in the world through lust.*

2 PETER 1:4

Have you noticed that there is corruption in the world through lust? But that fact need not bother us if we lean hard on the exceedingly great and precious promises of God that enable us to be partakers of the divine nature.

Promises are only effective if two conditions are met. The first is the character and reliability of the promiser. In this case, the Promiser, our Lord, is beyond reproach and utterly trustworthy. Second, the promise is nothing but dead words on the page until the message is believed and acted upon. We *have* the promise. Do we believe it? Then we must live it.

*"The tree of the promise will not drop its fruit
unless shaken by the hand of prayer."*

THOMAS WATSON

THE DEATH OF
THE OLD NATURE

*Reckon ye also yourselves to be dead indeed unto sin,
but alive unto God through Jesus Christ our Lord.*

ROMANS 6:11

I ronically, one of the most amazing and important promises for the believer is the one that declares us dead. Dead to sin, that is. The flip side of the promise grants us our freedom from sin as it declares us alive to God through Jesus Christ our Lord. This crucial promise enables us to overcome temptation.

Yes, we will continue to be tempted, but that part of us that responds positively to temptation is dead—and this fact becomes reality in our lives when we reckon it so and live it out in this temptation-filled world.

*"Are you alive? Then see that you prove it by your actions. Be
a consistent witness. Let your words, and works, and ways,
and tempers all tell the same story. Let not your life be a poor
torpid life, like that of a tortoise or a sloth—let it rather
be an energetic stirring life, like that of a deer or bird."*

J.C. RYLE

OUR ALL-SUFFICIENT GOD

Such trust have we through Christ to God-ward: not
that we are sufficient of ourselves to think any thing
as of ourselves; but our sufficiency is of God.

2 CORINTHIANS 3:4-5

Thank God we have been set free from "self-sufficiency." We knew long ago we were incomplete, insufficient, *lost*. But now we have made a marvelous trade. We have given our lack to God in exchange for His bountifulness. We are full of Christ, full of the Holy Spirit, leading a God-directed life. Our sufficiency is complete, anchored in the promises of God's Word. Our sufficiency now overflows, limited only by our capacity to believe and receive. Take note, though: We are only sufficient in those things that pertain to us. God does not supply sufficiency in areas in which He is not Lord.

"Our God has boundless resources. The only limit
is in us. Our asking, our thinking, our praying are
too small. Our expectations are too limited."

A.B. SIMPSON

BLESSINGS RUNNING OVER

Thou preparest a table before me
in the presence of mine enemies:
thou anointest my head with oil;
my cup runneth over.

PSALM 23:5

Where does God set His table of plenty? Right smack dab in the presence of our enemies. What better place! Our generous God makes it known to our enemies—particularly Satan—that He will not allow us to suffer defeat. And to put an exclamation mark to His provision, our Lord even fills our cup to overflowing! What then do we lack? If we trek through the wilderness, the table is still there and the cup still overflows. Best of all, He sups with us in the wilderness.

"It is no little comfort to be well and divinely assured that,
in whatever part of the wilderness your lot may be cast;
however weary and pressing your need, numerous and
potent your enemies, yet there the Shepherd has prepared a
table of the most appropriate and costly viands, and invites
you to partake, He Himself presiding at the banquet."

OCTAVIUS WINSLOW

NO LACK

The young lions do lack, and suffer hunger:
but they that seek the Lord shall not want any good thing.

PSALM 34:10

Among the many promises given to those who seek the Lord, surely one of the most comforting is that we shall not want any good thing.

Oh, we may say we want this or that "good thing," but if we allow God to decide which are the good things we truly need, we'll happily find our good things are really few in number and other imagined good things are easily dispensed with.

Sometimes when we give up the good things we thought we needed, we suddenly find room for the good things God has appointed for us. The key is that we continue to seek the Lord and that we're obedient to the call on our life. Where God leads, God supplies.

"God's work done in God's way
will never lack God's supplies."

HUDSON TAYLOR

MORE BLESSINGS
ARE ON THEIR WAY

Surely goodness and mercy shall follow me
all the days of my life: and I will dwell
in the house of the LORD for ever.

PSALM 23:6

I f you're like most people, you've probably moved several times during your life, with possibly more relocations to come. Isn't it good, then, to know that someday we will dwell in the house of the Lord forever? We need never move again—nor will we want to. But it gets even better for the believer: Until that day, goodness and mercy shall be our companions as we journey through life. Tonight, if you look behind you, you'll surely see goodness and mercy following!

"Shepherd of Israel, lead us, feed us, keep us, restore us, and fully
bless us! Receive us, welcome us, and make a home for us even
while below. Good and gracious God, help us to confide in you,
courageously to press onward in our homeward path, assured
that goodness and mercy shall follow us all the days of our life;
and that we shall dwell in the house of the Lord forever!"

JAMES SMITH

OUR EARTHLY HOME

We know that if our earthly house of this tabernacle
were dissolved, we have a building of God, an house
not made with hands, eternal in the heavens. For
in this we groan, earnestly desiring to be clothed
upon with our house which is from heaven.

2 CORINTHIANS 5:1-2

Those who don't know Christ may groan over many of life's difficulties, but believers groan differently. When we groan, it's an expression of our yearning for home—our *heavenly* home. Another difference is in the way we view death. Without Christ, death is a fearful subject not eagerly discussed, and certainly not anticipated with joy. But Christians have a hope that we shall live on beyond the grave—and that we already have a home waiting for us on the other side. Truly, for those who follow Christ, the best is yet to come! Happy is the Christian who groans for heaven!

"Let us not be afraid to meditate often on the subject of heaven,
and to rejoice in the prospect of good things to come....
Let us take comfort in the remembrance of the other side."

J.C. RYLE

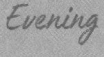

WHILE WAITING
FOR HEAVEN

After these things I heard a great voice of much people
in heaven, saying, Alleluia; salvation, and glory,
and honor, and power, unto the Lord our God.

REVELATION 19:1

The voices of praise coming from heaven never cease, for the worship of those departed is endless. And while we wait to join that heavenly choir, we can celebrate our longing by entering into heaven's praise: singing alleluias to God, worshipping our Lord, thanking Him for our future heavenly home, declaring Him worthy of our adoration. The praises we now begin on earth are but a taste of those to come in eternity.

If we listen closely, perhaps we can hear by faith those great voices of heaven now engaged in endless praise to which we will one day add our voice.

Ours is a happy and enduring yearning.

"Heaven is endless longing, accompanied with an endless
fruition—a longing which is blessedness, a longing which is life."
ALEXANDER MACLAREN

MIRACLES STILL HAPPEN

*The people with one accord gave heed unto
those things which Philip spake, hearing
and seeing the miracles which he did.*

ACTS 8:6

All of us at one time or another need a miracle. And God does grant miracles, though not often in the way we expect. True, there are "fast" miracles that change circumstances on the spot. But there are also "slow" miracles wherein God gently reveals His power on a day-by-day basis until the revelation is complete. We often get impatient with slow miracles, preferring an instant answer to our prayers. But in so doing, are we not, to some extent, usurping God's will? When we know the God of miracles, we can wait patiently for His work to bring about the needed miracle in due time—His time.

*"Believer! what can better support and sustain you amid the
trials of your pilgrimage, than the thought that you have an
Omnipotent arm to lean upon? The God with whom you
have to do, is boundless in His resources. There is no crossing
His designs, no thwarting His purposes, no questioning His
counsels. His mandate is law; He speaks, and it is done!"*

JOHN MACDUFF

MIRACLES TAKEN FOR GRANTED

Though he had done so many miracles before them,
yet they believed not on him.

JOHN 12:37

It's hard for us to imagine hearts so stony that onlookers who witnessed miracles would still disbelieve. But maybe we shouldn't be too hard on them. After all, truth be told, many of us have wondered if God would come through this time, even though we can recount the dozens of times in the past when He brought about a miracle to resolve an "impossible" trial.

Perhaps you're in the waiting room for a miracle from God. Can you be content if the waiting lasts a while longer, knowing that God's miracles are worth the wait?

Face it, our very life is a miracle. Our next breath is a miracle. Should we awake tomorrow morning, that, too, would be a miracle. We must never take God for granted, for all of life is a miracle.

"A Christian is a perpetual miracle."
CHARLES SPURGEON

GROW IN GRACE

*Grow in grace, and in the knowledge of our Lord and Savior
Jesus Christ. To him be glory both now and for ever. Amen.*

2 PETER 3:18

Our Christian life need not be static. In fact, we should always
be advancing, growing in grace. Yes, it may seem hard to
move forward in the light of what many consider reversals, whether
related to finances, relationships, or health. But it's in our difficulties
that God gives more grace—or it may seem that way. While we pray
for our health and for recovery from our setbacks, let's avail ourselves
of the opportunity for more growth and more grace.

Truth is, we already have more than enough grace. In addition
to growing in grace, we're also expected to grow in the knowledge
of our Lord and Savior. That closeness only comes as we draw near
to Him through prayer and through understanding more of Him
as we read and absorb His Word.

*"I am certain that I never did grow in grace one half so
much anywhere as I have upon the bed of pain."*

CHARLES SPURGEON

UNDER CONSTRUCTION

*Being confident of this very thing, that he
which hath begun a good work in you will
perform it until the day of Jesus Christ.*

PHILIPPIANS 1:6

Sometimes we're too hard on ourselves. We fail and beat ourselves up. Or we imagine that God is mad at us—or at the worst, even giving up on us.

The reality is that God has never started a work He didn't intend to finish. He started a good work in us, and He will see it through, regardless of our weaknesses and shortcomings. Every Bible hero had serious faults and failures, but God saw them through. He will see us through too. *We* may give up on incomplete projects, but God finishes His projects.

*"Let us take comfort in the thought that the Lord Jesus does
not cast off His believing people because of failures and
imperfections. He knows what they are…. He knew what
they were before conversion: wicked, guilty, and defiled;
yet He loved them. He knows what they will be after
conversion: weak, erring, and frail; yet He loves them. He
has undertaken to save them, notwithstanding all their
shortcomings and what He has undertaken, He will perform."*

J.C. RYLE

NOT WHAT I WAS

*Put off all these; anger, wrath, malice, blasphemy, filthy
communication out of your mouth. Lie not one to another,
seeing that ye have put off the old man with his deeds; and
have put on the new man, which is renewed in knowledge
after the image of him that created him.*

COLOSSIANS 3:8-10

When we're working on a project and it falters, we may try to do the best we can with the mess. Maybe a new paint job will cover the mistakes. Maybe no one will notice.

God has a different way of dealing with lives gone awry. He recognizes their unfixable status, and instead of new paint, He discards the old and starts a new work by giving the person a new nature. The old unfixable person is done away with, and like a potter who sees a cracked vessel on the wheel, the Lord removes the pieces and starts with fresh clay.

Today you are not who you're going to be in the future, but neither are you what you once were.

*"Conversion is a deep work, a heart work. It makes a new
man in a new world. It extends to the whole man: to the
mind, to the members, to the motions of the whole life."*

JOSEPH ALLEINE

TRANSFORMATION

Be not conformed to this world: but be ye transformed
by the renewing of your mind, that ye may prove what is
that good, and acceptable, and perfect, will of God.

ROMANS 12:2

Though God orders for us a new creation at our rebirth, He then gives us the means to bring the new creation into maturity through transformation. In our past life, now forsaken, we were molded by the world around us. Now we renew our being by allowing ourselves to be molded by the living and written Word of God.

This transformation affects every part of us—for every part of us needs salvation. And the goal of transformation is that we bear the likeness of Christ.

"Saving knowledge is a transforming knowledge, which
metamorphoses the soul. Divine light beating on the heart,
warms it, and betters it; it transforms and changes it, it
moulds and fashions it into the very likeness of Christ!"

THOMAS BROOKS

HARVEST IN DUE TIME

Let us not be weary in well doing: for in due season
we shall reap, if we faint not. As we have therefore
opportunity, let us do good unto all men, especially
unto them who are of the household of faith.

GALATIANS 6:9-10

You may have much to do today. Important items on your to-do list may be nipping at your heels. But God supplies the time and energy to do all that is important. What's crucial is that we keep on keeping on, that we not become weary in fighting the good fight or so consumed by our activities that we forget God.

Stay centered in Christ today, even if the list is long, even if others intrude or temptations arise. Stay the course today. You will reap a harvest if you spend your days aligned with God's purposes.

"Do not lose yourself in your everyday work and activities.
Rather, lose yourself in God. When you are doing work, let
your innermost heart be centered on Him. Live in His
presence and abide in Him. Then your work will follow
you into eternity, and you will reap a rich harvest."

BASILEA SCHLINK

A BOUNTIFUL HARVEST

He which soweth sparingly shall reap also sparingly;
and he which soweth bountifully shall reap also bountifully.

2 CORINTHIANS 9:6

We can scarcely expect fruit to grow on a pine tree. Nor should we look for apples on an orange tree. Fruit is born based on the inner life of the tree, and that inner life is based on the seed that was planted. If we want an apple tree, we best plant apple seeds.

Since we're believers, God has called us to sow seeds of the gospel as we go through life—both in our deeds and in our words.

Tonight as you retire, ask God's blessing on the seed you've sown recently. Expect a harvest—a bountiful harvest. Herein is the Father glorified.

> *"The man who prays for a bountiful harvest but prepares*
> *no ground and plants no seed will pray in vain. Faith and*
> *works must go together. We must submit to God to 'direct'*
> *our efforts and 'command' our efforts. We must be willing*
> *to work when he wants us to work—and in the way*
> *he wants us to work. Our attempts to trust will*
> *amount to nothing if we are not willing to obey."*
>
> CHARLES NAYLOR

A CROWN AWAITS

When the chief Shepherd shall appear,
ye shall receive a crown of glory that fadeth not away.
1 PETER 5:4

Someday when Christ appears, we shall each receive a crown that cannot be taken from us, that will not fade away. We shall go from being servants here on earth to royalty in heaven. The reward is to the faithful, and faithful we shall be, our Lord having first proved His faithfulness to us time after time.

Yes, we will wear crowns in eternity, but we will lay them at the feet of the King of kings. Until then, let our earthly crowns be the works we perform as lights in a dark world.

"God hath in Himself all power to defend you,
all wisdom to direct you, all mercy to pardon you,
all grace to enrich you, all righteousness to
clothe you, all goodness to supply you,
and all happiness to crown you."
THOMAS BROOKS

STAYING THE COURSE

*I am now ready to be offered, and the time of my
departure is at hand. I have fought a good fight,
I have finished my course, I have kept the faith:
Henceforth there is laid up for me a crown of
righteousness, which the Lord, the righteous judge,
shall give me at that day: and not to me only,
but unto all them also that love his appearing.*

2 TIMOTHY 4:6-8

Do we love His appearing? Or does it frighten us? We need have
no fear of Christ's return. It is for *us* that He returns. And He
will bring all those believers who remain alive home to live with
Him in eternity.

Then our Father God will give us crowns that He made Himself.
The glory of heaven will be living with our true King in harmony
with heaven's hosts.

*"Sin has made us our crosses;
God has made us our crown."*

THOMAS WATSON

BELIEVING IS SEEING

We walk by faith, not by sight.
2 CORINTHIANS 5:7

How easy it would be if we were to walk by sight. Or would it? Walking by faith necessitates trusting God when we can't see Him working—and that's a good thing. God wants a people who fully believe, trust, and rely on Him even though His presence is not seen. Walking by faith proves our commitment to our invisible God.

If we were walking by sight, we might alternately fear what we see in our circumstances, rather than trust God in the midst of trials. Walking by sight, we would have no need for faith—the very quality God approves.

We all walk by faith today because we must and because God has planned it that way. But never fear: The reward of walking by faith is to see what we have believed as God's unseen hand rewards our blind trust.

> *"Faith is to believe what we do not see, and the*
> *reward of this faith is to see what we believe."*
> AUGUSTINE

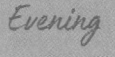

FULL-ON TRUST

The LORD is my rock, and my fortress, and my deliverer;
my God, my strength, in whom I will trust; my buckler,
and the horn of my salvation, and my high tower.

PSALM 18:2

It's so easy to trust God in the small things of life. We barely need any faith at all. But for the big things, well, that's a different story. We quiver at the prospect of loss arising from our trials. We worry about finances, health, jobs, and more. We try to imagine having faith, but our fear wins out.

David went through many trials—often life-threatening—and yet he was a friend of God and a man of faith (*despite* his fears). Whatever your current situation, embrace it in full-on trust. Let the Lord be your rock, fortress, and deliverer. Run to Him as your high tower.

"Take the very hardest thing in your life, the place of difficulty,
outward or inward, and expect God to triumph gloriously in
that very spot. Just there He can bring your soul into blossom."

LILIAS TROTTER

READY OR NOT...

*Sanctify the Lord God in your hearts: and be ready always
to give an answer to every man that asketh you a reason
of the hope that is in you with meekness and fear.*

1 PETER 3:15

Have you ever been given an unexpected opportunity to share your faith, only to come up with the right words *after* the chance to share has passed? Sometimes we're just caught up short. We think, "If only I had known ahead of time, I could have been prepared with the perfect answer."

One way to avoid these disappointments is to prepare a good answer for almost any query ahead of time. This often will involve simply having an example to share about how God has worked in your life. After all, no one can refute your firsthand experience.

Can you now bring to mind ways God has been faithful to you that might help someone else? One doesn't need a degree in apologetics to give a right answer. We just need experience with the Lord and the words to share how God has worked in our lives.

*"We should be able to defend our religion
with meekness, in the fear of God."*

MATTHEW HENRY

I'VE GOT THIS!

Verily, verily, I say unto you, He that believeth on me,
the works that I do shall he do also; and greater works
than these shall he do; because I go unto my Father.

JOHN 14:12

When Christ ascended into heaven, He left us the promise of doing greater works than He did. That's quite a hefty promise. It's also a major responsibility. God often brings people into our lives for the express purpose of allowing us to minister to them. We might have just the right words to share or perhaps the opportunity to pray with someone—or even lead them to Christ.

No matter what our "greater work" might be, it must be rooted and supported by prayer and strong faith. God will use us in proportion to our faith. Therefore it behooves us to pray for opportunities to do our greater works—and for the faith to follow through. When we do, we find great joy in having been used by God to help somebody.

"If there are great battles and great works to do, there
must be great faith. Assurance can carry mountains
on its back; little faith stumbles at a mole-hill."

CHARLES SPURGEON

GOD IS AHEAD OF US

The Lord will perfect that which concerneth me:
thy mercy, O Lord, endureth for ever:
forsake not the works of thine own hands.

PSALM 138:8

We are each a creation of God. We are *His*, and He takes care of His workmanship. We can rightly affirm along with the psalmist, "The Lord will perfect that which concerneth me." Thus, we are not left to the whims of chance. God knows no happenstance, no such thing as "luck," nor does He allow our enemies within and without to thwart His work in us. Be at peace, for He will not forsake the work of His hands.

"As You have made me, teach me. Here I am, the vessel which You
have made; Lord, fill it! You have given me both soul and body.
Grant me now Your grace that my soul may know Your will, and
my body can join in performing it. The plea is very forcible and
magnifies the cry, Forsake not the works of your own hands."

CHARLES SPURGEON

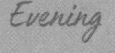
GREAT AND MIGHTY

Call unto me, and I will answer thee, and show thee
great and mighty things, which thou knowest not.

JEREMIAH 33:3

Does God call each of us to see and even participate in great and mighty things? The truth is, if we could see His perfect plan for our life, we'd see a unique design that both fulfills God's will for us and grants us happiness. But we'd also see the many times we veered off the course and how God then took our errors and even sins and redeemed our history to show us great and mighty things we knew not.

After Jesus ascended into heaven, He left behind disciples who were flawed but who still saw great and mighty things—and also did those great and mighty things. And so will we. Indeed, every work of God in our life is great and mighty.

"Hope in God, for he will do as he has said; yes, he will
do exceeding abundantly above all we can ask or think.
He will make all his goodness pass before us, and show
us great and mighty things which we know not."

JAMES SMITH

187

WISDOM—THE SOURCE OF HAPPINESS

Happy is the man that findeth wisdom,
and the man that getteth understanding.

PROVERBS 3:13

We live in a day in which knowledge abounds, but wisdom is scarce. Someone has correctly said that wisdom is the ability to apply knowledge rightly. Knowledge, then, requires wisdom in order to be useful. And wisdom applied to our lives brings happiness, for even in dark times, wisdom looks ahead for the positive outcome of the trial. Thus, if we would be happy, truly happy, we must first become wise and "get understanding."

"The yoke of Wisdom is easy, her burden is light. To find the Wisdom of God is to find rest to the soul, light to the eyes, and joy to the heart. To find Wisdom (Christ) is to find the holy, blissful, all-conquering will, and mercy of God. A man cannot make such a find without being renewed in the whole inner man."

JAMES SMITH

HAPPY IS THAT PEOPLE

Thou wilt show me the path of life:
in thy presence is fulness of joy; at thy
right hand there are pleasures forevermore.

PSALM 16:11

Who among us doesn't want to be happy? Anyone may enjoy happy moments, glad weeks and months, even some joyful years. But long-term happiness requires the knowledge of God. Indeed, undergirding all true happiness is the presence of the Lord. For in His presence, there is no sorrow that cannot be healed, no disappointment that cannot be made right, no broken relationship that cannot be mended. It's only as we remove ourselves from the knowledge of God that happiness recedes. Making God the Lord of our life reverses even the worst adversity.

Just ask Job.

"God is the donor of all true happiness.
God is the maintainer of all true happiness.
God is the center of all true happiness and blessedness.
Therefore, he who has Him for his God, for his portion,
is the only happy man in the world!"

THOMAS BROOKS

FELLOWSHIP

*Where two or three are gathered together
in my name, there am I in the midst of them.*

MATTHEW 18:20

Many Christians miss out on God's best when they avoid fellowship with other believers. In truth, we were not built to travel through life alone. God gives many of us mates for life, but He gives all of us believers other brothers and sisters to join with us in prayer, to bear our burdens with us, and to comfort us in our trials.

For most of us, simply going to church once a week, with perhaps a midweek Bible study thrown in, isn't enough. We need more than that. We need deeper Christian friendships.

Who are your primary Christian friends? Are they supporting you in your needs? Are you supporting them? If the answer is no, prayerfully seek out others who need what you have and are able to give you what they have. You may be surprised at how many Lone Ranger Christians would love to have deeper fellowship with other believers.

*"In all our proceedings we should seek direction in prayer;
we cannot too highly prize the promises of God. Wherever
and whenever we meet in the name of Christ, we
should consider him as present in the midst of us."*

MATTHEW HENRY

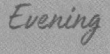

ASSEMBLING TOGETHER

Not forsaking the assembling of ourselves together,
as the manner of some is; but exhorting one another:
and so much the more, as ye see the day approaching.

HEBREWS 10:25

If, as many Christians suspect, hard times are ahead as we "see the day approaching," it will be all the more important to be part of a mature and continually growing fellowship of believers. Simply put, we will need each other more than ever.

The good news is that God has promised to be in the midst of such congregations, and where God is, there are always blessings. One stated purpose of corporate worship is that we can exhort one another—building one another up to endure hard times with joy.

The Christian who has found his or her spiritual home in a good fellowship of believers is blessed indeed.

"The Lord is always present in the assembly of the
saints, and present on purpose to bless them."

JAMES SMITH

AMAZING GRACE,
HOW SWEET THE SOUND

Sin shall not have dominion over you:
for ye are not under the law, but under grace.

ROMANS 6:14

It's no wonder that "Amazing Grace" has been the most popular hymn of all time. The message is clear: God's grace to sinful man *is* simply amazing. Even more, we all know how much we need a grace that amazes us. To begin your day, read and absorb again the first three stanzas of this amazing hymn.

"Amazing grace! How sweet the sound that saved a wretch like me!
I once was lost, but now am found; was blind, but now I see.
Through many dangers, toils and snares I have already come;
'Tis grace hath brought me safe thus far, and grace will lead me home.
The Lord has promised good to me, His Word my hope secures;
He will my Shield and Portion be, as long as life endures."

JOHN NEWTON

WHEN WE'VE BEEN THERE TEN THOUSAND YEARS

A voice came out of the throne, saying,
Praise our God, all ye his servants,
and ye that fear him, both small and great.

REVELATION 19:5

Hopefully, the words and tune to "Amazing Grace" have stuck with you throughout the day. But there's much more to this hymn, and in the final two stanzas, we focus not on God's grace in this mortal life but on life eternal.

Tonight, as you retire, allow these words to be your last thoughts.

"The earth shall soon dissolve like snow, the sun forbear to shine;
But God, who called me here below, will be forever mine.
When we've been there ten thousand years, bright shining as the sun,
We've no less days to sing God's praise than when we'd first begun."

JOHN NEWTON

A HEALTHY THOUGHT LIFE

As he thinketh in his heart, so is he.

PROVERBS 23:7

How is your thought life today?

Whatever your answer, you will likely act based on how you think. In various places, the Bible addresses the human mind and its thoughts. We're told to renew our minds, to think on things of good report, to take captive evil thoughts.

In truth, our behavior follows our thoughts. If you need to change any aspect of your behavior, change first your thoughts. This comes through a disciplining of how we think. We must practice changing our minds—not an easy task, given all the years of conditioning we've gone through, conditioning that tempts us to center ourselves on the world or self rather than on Christ.

Just as we must take care what goes into our body, so too must we recondition our minds to think as God thinks. We must learn how to reject inappropriate thoughts and how to say yes to edifying thoughts. You will have an opportunity today to implement this practice. Don't overlook it.

"The man is as the mind is."

THOMAS BROOKS

REFUSING IMPURE THOUGHTS

Brethren, whatsoever things are true,
whatsoever things are honest, whatsoever things are just,
whatsoever things are pure, whatsoever things are lovely,
whatsoever things are of good report; if there be any virtue,
and if there be any praise, think on these things.

PHILIPPIANS 4:8

The apostle Paul tells us how to think. We can thus choose our thoughts, rather than allow our minds to be open to every fleeting suggestion from Satan or self.

Tonight, as you rest from the day, choose a time to specifically name some true, honest, just, pure, lovely thoughts of good report. These are your ammunition when tempted to evil or destructive thoughts.

"Much of the gloomy tinge which many people see on everything,
is caused by the color of the glasses through which they look. We
put on our blue glasses, and then wonder what makes everything
blue and dismal. The greater part of our discontent is caused
by some imaginary trouble, which never really comes. Fix
your thoughts on what is true and honorable and right. Think
about things that are pure and lovely and admirable. Think
about things that are excellent and worthy of praise."

J.R. MILLER

FAITHFUL IN OUR EARTHLY ROLES

We are his workmanship, created in Christ Jesus
unto good works, which God hath before ordained
that we should walk in them.

EPHESIANS 2:10

Believers are called not to a random life but to a specific type of work. It can be as simple (and yet profound) as intercession, or as public as evangelism or teaching Bible studies. In truth, knowing that we've been called and knowing what that calling is gives us great confidence and joy to be part of God's work.

Whatever your assignment is, know that God has worked—and *is* working—circumstances to bring you favor in your calling. Yes, He is ahead of us on the path, showing the way, clearing the obstacles that would slow us down.

We need only to follow Him.

"God has foreordained the works to which He has called
you. He has been ahead of you preparing the place to
which you are coming and manipulating all the resources
of the universe in order that the work you do may be
a part of His whole great and gracious work."

G. CAMPBELL MORGAN

POWER TO BECOME SONS OF GOD

As many as received him, to them gave he power to become the sons of God, even to them that believe on his name.

JOHN 1:12

When God called us to Himself, we said yes. He then empowered us supernaturally to become His sons and daughters. All it took was that yes from us.

Now, having become a child of God, each of us is also given a work to do while on earth. But the fact is, not all works are the same. Some are very simple, others more detailed.

And how do we know our assignment? By recognizing what we're good at (our gifts), by letting God's Word speak to us, by receiving the affirmation of mature Christians who know us well, and by noticing the way circumstances have unfolded in our lives. Most Christians are called to some sort of secular work, which often gives them the ability to support full-time workers for the Lord. But even those with a secular job may have a work to do on the side. That, too, can be discovered by the steps above.

"Do we desire to be sons of God? Then let us receive Christ as our Savior, and believe on Him with the heart. To every one that so receives Him, He will give the privilege of becoming a son of God."

J.C. RYLE

LISTENING FOR THE STILL, SMALL VOICE

After the earthquake a fire;
but the LORD was not in the fire:
and after the fire a still small voice.

1 KINGS 19:12

We do not choose how God will speak to us. So we listen. Sometimes we hear His voice very clearly. But other times, when He speaks in a still, small voice, we must listen very, very closely to hear Him. How will you hear Him today?

"In every event, important or trivial in the estimation of man, he speaks and says 'It is I!' In poverty, 'It is I!' In sickness, 'It is I!' In anxiety, 'It is I!' In bereavement, 'It is I!' Whatever be the nature of the storm, from whatever quarter the hurricane may blow, still Jesus says, 'It is I!'…Even then amid the gloom, may Jesus be seen by the eye of faith, walking in majesty upon the waves and, amid the elemental din, His 'still small voice' of mingled dignity and love may be heard saying, 'It is I; do not be afraid.'"

NEWMAN HALL

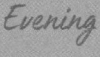
ATTUNING OUR EARS, TRAINING OUR MOUTH

*My beloved brethren, let every man be swift to hear,
slow to speak, slow to wrath. For the wrath of man
worketh not the righteousness of God.*

JAMES 1:19-20

When God speaks in a still, small voice, we must listen closely. James tells us to be swift to hear—and slow to speak. As we tune our ears to His voice, let's also train our mouth to be slow to speak. Much damage has been done by mouths too eager to speak. Churches have split, relationships ended, families broken apart—all because of the unruly mouth.

Tonight, let your prayer be for listening ears and a disciplined mouth.

"Jesus never spoke a hasty word. He kept silent under insult, pain, reproach, and sorest injury—not sullen silence—but silence sweet with patient, peaceful love. We are never sorry for following this perfect example, and restraining the cutting words."

J.R. MILLER

OBEDIENCE

Behold, to obey is better than sacrifice,
and to hearken than the fat of rams.
1 SAMUEL 15:22

God values obedience in His children—so much so that He values it far above the required Old Testament sacrifices.

And our best obedience as we go along in life is moving ahead with God, not standing still. He is, after all, a forward-thinking God, so to obey is to move ahead. To disobey, on the other hand, is to lag behind.

How do we obey? We simply do what we know God wants us to do. It may mean beginning something, changing something, or ending something. And for most of us, the latter—ending something—is the hardest of the three.

For instance, if we're dealing with addiction or if we're given to anger or selfishness, ending that behavior can be difficult. But no matter which obedience is required of us, we must comply or be left behind in the dust.

"Trust God and do the next thing."
OSWALD CHAMBERS

THE DELICIOUS
FRUIT OF OBEDIENCE

If ye be willing and obedient,
ye shall eat the good of the land.

ISAIAH 1:19

We obey because that's what servants do—and we are servants of God. The irony is that unlike most servants, we are blessed when we obey. In truth, concealed within every directive of God there is hidden blessing. And those who refuse to obey, or who do so reluctantly, will miss the blessing.

Are you confident of your obedience to God's directives for your life? Search your heart tonight. Ask yourself, "Is my walk with God a walk of obedience...or is there something the Holy Spirit is nudging me to do?"

As you end the evening, resolve to obey God cheerfully, swiftly, and without reluctance. And remember that the blessing within the obedience awaits you.

"That is the best obedience, which is cheerful, as that
is the sweetest honey which drops out of the comb.
Obey God swiftly.... Obey the King of glory."

THOMAS WATSON

SLOW TO ANGER

The Lord is merciful and gracious,
slow to anger, and plenteous in mercy.

PSALM 103:8

Have you ever felt like God was angry with you? Though it's true that anger is one of God's many emotions, His anger is focused on sin and its effects on His creation—so much so that He provided a gospel that brings the good news of forgiveness of sins. Simply put, the righteous anger of God toward our sin was directed instead to Christ. He bore the wrath of God for our sins. Thus, in dealing with us now, God is full of mercy and grace—and He is slow, not quick, to anger.

So now the question is, are we also slow to anger and full of mercy and grace toward others? If so, we exhibit one of God's great character qualities. Make anger one of your lesser emotions. And if anger is called for, resolve the issue quickly. Don't let it fester. That's not God's way.

"Our God is not an impotent God with one arm; but
as he is slow to anger, so is he great in power."

ABRAHAM WRIGHT

BE ANGRY AND SIN NOT

Be ye angry, and sin not:
let not the sun go down upon your wrath.

EPHESIANS 4:26

Human anger is not a sinful emotion. Yes, it can lead to sin, but anger can also work toward resolving injustice.

Godly anger is anger that is rare, that is focused on righting an injustice and is under the person's control. Uncontrolled anger, however, is not a valid response to any situation. Nor is anger that provokes violence. And seething anger that stays under the surface for a long time is also not valid. In short, godly anger seeks resolution; it does not revel in simmering for days or weeks, for months or years.

Scripture admonishes us to deal with our anger the same day the troubling situation occurs. Tonight, perhaps you can relax unangered, but take it to heart that your evenings should never conclude with unresolved anger, so long as it is in your power to end it. See if forgiveness or compromise isn't a more appropriate action.

"Anger is short-lived in a good man."

THOMAS FULLER

WALK IN THE SPIRIT

*Walk in the Spirit, and ye shall
not fulfil the lust of the flesh.*

GALATIANS 5:16

We always have two options—and only two. We can walk in the Spirit—under His control and bearing the fruit of the Spirit—or we can walk according to the flesh with all its attendant "fruits."

A life built on walking in the Spirit daily will result in a good life, while a fleshly walk will result in anguish, bitterness, and tears.

Simply put, there is Holy Spirit power behind "walking in the Spirit." Circumstances can even bend to the good of the Spirit-led Christian. And a bonus to walking in the Spirit is that we display to others the advantages of a Christ-filled life.

> *"In this walking after the Spirit lies much, if not all, of the
> power of godliness. Nor indeed is there any real happiness or
> comfort without it. For immediately that we cease to walk
> after the Spirit, we walk after the flesh, we lose our evidences,
> we can no longer see our signs, and all the sweet promises of
> the gospel and our interest in them are hidden from view."*
>
> J.C. PHILPOT

THE SPIRIT ABIDES

He that keepeth his commandments dwelleth in him,
and he in him. And hereby we know that he abideth in us,
by the Spirit which he hath given us.

1 JOHN 3:24

There is only one way God recognizes His children: Do they have the Holy Spirit within? Do they display a Spirit-led distinction from the rest of the world? The Holy Spirit has been described in the Bible as a "seal" and as a "mark." We are sealed by God as His own children. We are marked by God as sheep selected from the flock for the Shepherd's keeping.

Tonight, if you must count sheep to fall asleep, count yourself wearing a blue ribbon. You have won first prize.

"The indwelling of God the Holy Spirit is the common mark
of all true believers in Christ. It is the Shepherd's mark on
the flock of the Lord Jesus, distinguishing them from the
rest of the world. It is the goldsmith's stamp on the genuine
sons of God, which separates them from the dross and mass
of false professors. It is the King's own seal on those who are
His peculiar people, proving them to be His own property....
This is the case of all believers. They all have the Spirit."

J.C. RYLE

THE BATTLE IS THE LORD'S

The LORD strong and mighty,
the LORD mighty in battle.

PSALM 24:8

Our God is a warrior, strong and mighty. He fights our battles for us, knowing we have no power or might of our own. Blessed is the Christian who has given up fighting for self and has handed the sword over to God.

Are you facing a battle today at work or home? Is depression or some negative emotion your foe? Or perhaps you're confronting another person, or maybe a severe temptation.

Know that God allows for each of us unique battles, conflicts that when won by trusting in the Lord, strong and mighty, help us mature in our faith. We never rest entirely from the battles of this life, for there is always need for a deeper, more mature faith.

Today, be wise enough to give up your own feeble fight and let God handle the situation. After all, He's never lost a battle.

"There is no use fighting the battle in our
own strength. We have none."

J.C. PHILPOT

THE VICTORY IS OURS!

All this assembly shall know that the LORD saveth
not with sword and spear: for the battle is the LORD's,
and he will give you into our hands.

1 SAMUEL 17:47

Though the battle is the Lord's, the fruits of victory belong to us. It's as if God, winning the battle on our behalf, then awards the victory to us. Oh, He won it, to be sure. But He did so for us.

Each battle won adds to the previous line of victories, and one day we shall look back at our history and see that our Christian life owes its happiness to the faithfulness of God in battle.

"To afflictions, a natural man can oppose stoical endurance; to temptation, a hardened conscience; to doubts, impenitence, or self-righteousness; to attacks from men, blow for blow. But all these weapons have dropped from a Christian's hand; God must fight his battles, for he cannot. He has therefore no power, nor wisdom, nor strength, nor might against this great company, for his weapons are not carnal, but spiritual; so that if he fights, it must be in the strength of the Lord, and the power of His might."

J.C. PHILPOT

GOD'S OPEN HAND

Thou openest thine hand,
and satisfiest the desire of every living thing.

Psalm 145:16

Two hands must be opened to receive from God. First, His hand is opened to dispense needed blessings on our behalf. But if our hand is not also open, if our palm is not exposed, we cannot receive what the Lord has for us. Would we dare miss today's blessing because of our closed fist? God is at the ready to dispense all we need for today, but we must open our clenched fingers to receive.

Will you today open your hand and receive a blessing from God? His hand is ready to give. And then, after you've received, will you open your hand to give to others? We receive the divine blessings, but then we pass them on, thus becoming a channel of blessing.

"If we be empty and poor, it is not because God's
hand is straitened, but ours is not opened."

Thomas Manton

GOD'S HIDDEN HAND

*Can a woman forget her sucking child, that she
should not have compassion on the son of her womb?
yea, they may forget, yet will I not forget thee. Behold,
I have graven thee upon the palms of my hands;
thy walls are continually before me.*

ISAIAH 49:15-16

If we could see the palm of God's hand, we'd see our name inscribed on it. More than inscribed, it's *engraved*. How permanent is an engraving? It certainly lasts longer than the writing of any pen or marker. That's why we use engravings to ensure the memory of loved ones.

Though we may forget our duties to a loved one out of carelessness, God never forgets. His palm, hidden from us, is evidence of His open love for us.

*"Child of God, let your cheerful eyes and your joyful
heart testify how great a wonder it is that you, once so
vile, so hard of heart, so far estranged from God, are
this day written on the palms of his hands!"*

CHARLES SPURGEON

OWNED BY GOD

*Thus saith the Lord that created thee, O Jacob, and he that
formed thee, O Israel, Fear not: for I have redeemed thee,
I have called thee by thy name; thou art mine.*

ISAIAH 43:1

As our Creator and Redeemer, God alone has the right to call us His own. Yes, we are *owned* by God. We are His prized possession. As His children, we inherit all that is our Father's. He gives us access to blessings freely. But He also can do with us as He will. That may include a few trials and temptations throughout life, but as with all owners, God can bring an end to them in His own good time.

Throughout the day, carry with you the knowledge that you do not belong to yourself, your employer, or even your mate. Our God is jealous over you. He claims total possession.

> *"He is our absolute owner. No one can justly question
> his right, or interfere with his disposal of us. He may
> do as he will, with his own. But as infinitely wise,
> whatever he does will reflect his wisdom…. He will act
> wisely, justly, and in accordance with his mercy."*
>
> JAMES SMITH

GOD MAINTAINS
HIS POSSESSIONS

*The Lord is faithful, who shall stablish you,
and keep you from evil.*

2 THESSALONIANS 3:3

A wise person takes care of their possessions, especially those that are valuable. And God is no slacker when it comes to maintaining what is His. With His eyes upon us, He knows when to send blessing and when to delay it. He knows which trials will benefit us and which would destroy us. He sends gladness, and He sends sadness. He deals with each of His treasured ones with individual concern. In short, there is no matter concerning us that is too small for Him to notice and tend to. It is a good thing to acknowledge God's ownership each day, to remember that we are merely the pot on the potter's wheel, not the potter himself.

*"Our God is great—but He knows our names and loves
us individually, the least as tenderly as the greatest. His
guardianship extends also to all our life, to the most
insignificant circumstances and experiences."*

J.R. MILLER

GO UP HIGHER

When thou art bidden, go and sit down in the lowest room;
that when he that bade thee cometh, he may say unto thee,
Friend, go up higher: then shalt thou have worship
in the presence of them that sit at meat with thee.

LUKE 14:10

The way God's kingdom works is often upside down from this world's way of thinking. We're taught to promote ourselves, maybe brag about our accomplishments, schmooze with the people who can help us. But God's way up is down. If we want to be great in His kingdom, we will become servants. If we would truly live, we must die. If we wish to receive, we must give.

Learn to live by and enjoy God's upside-down plan for success. You really don't want success according to the way of the world.

"Let us not covet the highest place; let us not desire honor among
men. In the Church of God the way upward is downward. He
who will do the lowest work shall have the highest honor."

CHARLES SPURGEON

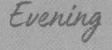

HUMBLING OURSELVES

Whosoever exalteth himself shall be abased;
and he that humbleth himself shall be exalted.

LUKE 14:11

We all have opportunities to exalt ourselves, perhaps by a talent we have or a special skill we've learned. But we should pass up those chances if the result is a prideful attitude. And if we can humbly acknowledge that our gifts come from God, that He gets the glory for our successes and abilities, so much the better.

The fact is, our natural inclination may be to watch for ways to exalt ourselves, but we can instead train ourselves to watch for ways to practice humility. If we don't, rest assured God has His ways of humbling us—and that for our own good.

In truth, when we really know ourselves, it's easy to be humble, for we all have much to be humble about and little to be prideful about.

> *"Humility may well be called the queen of the Christian*
> *graces. To know our own sinfulness and weakness, and to*
> *feel our need of Christ is the start of saving religion."*
>
> J.C. RYLE

SILENCING YOUR INNER CRITIC

*I heard a loud voice saying in heaven, Now is come
salvation, and strength, and the kingdom of our God, and
the power of his Christ: for the accuser of our brethren is cast
down, which accused them before our God day and night.*

REVELATION 12:10

We often judge ourselves too lightly or too harshly. In the former case, we may allow sin in our lives because we know we're under grace. In the latter case, we may accept Satan's ongoing accusations of failures as he confronts us with shortcomings that God forgave and forgot long ago.

But rest assured that God is our judge, not Satan and not ourselves. And God has justified us. Today, don't let yourself off the hook too easily if there's sin in your life. But be sure to silence the voice of the enemy when he accuses you. God has already rendered us "not guilty" by virtue of Christ's sacrifice. Stay free from condemnation.

*"Satan may accuse, but it is God that justifies!... Who will
dare condemn the soul whom He justifies? How gloriously
will this truth shine forth in the great day of judgment!
Every accuser will then be dumb. Every tongue will then be
silent. Nothing shall be laid to the charge of God's elect. God
Himself shall pronounce them fully and forever justified."*

OCTAVIUS WINSLOW

LISTENING TO YOUR
CLOUD OF CHEERLEADERS

*Wherefore seeing we also are compassed about with
so great a cloud of witnesses, let us lay aside every weight,
and the sin which doth so easily beset us, and let us
run with patience the race that is set before us.*

HEBREWS 12:1

Most of us have sins that we succumb to more readily, that sneak up on us and "so easily beset us." Yes, we have tried to overcome, but we have failed countless times. Even so, these sins must not be allowed to remain in our lives. All known sin must be dealt with by repentance, confession, and a faithful appropriating of God's forgiveness.

The writer of Hebrews encourages us in this setting aside of sin and weights by reminding us of the great cloud of witnesses who have gone on before us. They who now reside in heaven also once knew the weight of besetting sins, but they overcame their wrongdoings, and so can we. Best to overcome the small transgressions before they give way to larger, more enslaving sins.

*"Wickedness comes to its height by degrees. He that
dares say of a less sin, Is it not a little one? will ere
long say of a greater, Tush, God regards it not!"*

ANNE BRADSTREET

THIS FAR BY FAITH

Whatsoever is born of God overcometh the world: and
this is the victory that overcometh the world, even our faith.

1 JOHN 5:4

If we would overcome the obstacles in life, we must do so *by faith*. All our victories are by faith; all our losses are due to doubt. Can we today affirm that we have the necessary faith to overcome the world and its well-designed snares?

Remember, faith isn't just the way to overcome. Faith *is* overcoming. Nothing you will encounter today can bring you down unless you allow it. In the face of disappointment or adversity, have faith. Have the kind of confident trust that overcomes sin, defies Satan, dissolves perplexities, lifts us above our trials, separates us from the world, and conquers the fear of even death.

"We must learn to live on the heavenly side and look at
things from above. To contemplate all things as God sees
them, as Christ beholds them, overcomes sin, defies Satan,
dissolves perplexities, lifts us above trials, separates us
from the world and conquers fear of death."

A.B. SIMPSON

GOING ON IN FAITH

Let us hold fast the profession of our faith
without wavering; (for he is faithful that promised).
HEBREWS 10:23

To be sure, our faith can be challenged—and it often is. But God calls us to the kind of faith that cannot waver. This unwavering trust is an anchor to the soul. In the face of trouble, it doesn't tremble or run away. Indeed, God's brand of faith faces life's challenges head-on and wins.

We may have tried other means of overcoming adversity. And positive thinking, compromise, denial, and procrastination are just a few of the weaker strategies we employ. But the true ticket to victory is unwavering faith.

"You have had many a tossing up and down, and have
often needed a foothold for your faith to stand upon. You
have tried to believe this or that doctrine, or to get into
this or that experience; but you kept still falling short, for
you found that…you needed a solid foundation on which
to build for eternity; for the things to be believed were so
invisible and so mysterious, that nothing but the word of
God could suffice for your faith to stand upon and rest in."
J.C. PHILPOT

OUR TONGUE

The tongue is a little member, and boasteth great things.
Behold, how great a matter a little fire kindleth!

JAMES 3:5

The members of our body are often the worst perpetrators of sin. Notably, our tongue frequently gets us in trouble—it's a small member, to be sure, but capable of much danger. Who among us has not regretted our words, even before we finished speaking them? The apostle James is right to note that a small matter emblazoned by an unruly tongue can result in mayhem.

With this in mind, we would do well every morning to recommit our tongue to the Lord for that day. Then as the day progresses, we can monitor the thoughts that may lead to regrettable words. For words once spoken cannot be easily taken back.

Today limit your tongue to speaking good thoughts.

"Learn to hold thy tongue; five words cost
Zacharias forty weeks of silence."

THOMAS FULLER

OUR EYES

I will set no wicked thing before mine eyes.
Psalm 101:3

We live in a time when assaults to the eyes can come upon us unexpectedly. A billboard, a TV program, a scantily dressed member of the opposite sex—any of these can send our thoughts to a dark place that might lead us to entertain illicit images—or worse, act out on those impure thoughts. Training our eyes to look away from evil will save us many a sorrow.

"There was a little potted rose-bush in a sick-room which I visited. It sat by the window. One day I noticed that the one rose on the bush was looking toward the light. I referred to it, and the sick woman said that her daughter had turned the rose around several times toward the darkness of the room but that each time the little flower had twisted itself back, until again its face was toward the light. It would not look into the darkness. The rose taught me a lesson: never to allow myself to look toward any evil, but instantly to turn from it. Not a moment should we permit our eyes to be inclined toward anything sinful. To yield to one moment's sinful act, is to defile the soul."

J.R. Miller

WEAKNESS IS OUR STRENGTH

I take pleasure in infirmities, in reproaches, in necessities,
in persecutions, in distresses for Christ's sake:
for when I am weak, then am I strong.

2 CORINTHIANS 12:10

Few of us take pleasure in our weaknesses, as the apostle Paul did. Instead, we may try to hide our shortcomings or make up for them in other areas. But what really prevents us from echoing Paul's confession of weakness? Do we not believe that in our weakness God is able to impute His strength? We may have discovered that God doesn't bless our puny strength and make it stronger. No, He wants us to divest ourselves of our strength and admit our weakness precisely so that His strength in our life will prevail.

"Do not strive in your own strength; cast yourself at the
feet of the Lord Jesus, and wait upon Him in the sure
confidence that He is with you, and works in you. Strive
in prayer; let faith fill your heart—so will you be strong
in the Lord, and in the power of His might."

ANDREW MURRAY

QUIET CONFIDENCE

Thus saith the Lord GOD, the Holy One of Israel;
In returning and rest shall ye be saved; in quietness and
in confidence shall be your strength: and ye would not.

ISAIAH 30:15

*Q*uiet, calmness, weakness—these are words we rarely think of in terms of getting stuff done. We're more likely to noisily go about our tasks in our own strength, often rushing from one thing to another. But if God is the source of our strength, we can slow down and calmly expect Him to work methodically through us.

After all, God doesn't see time the same way we view it. God has always taken His time to bring about His will. Can we not do the same?

The words of God through the prophet Isaiah are very telling. The Lord had promised rest, quietness, confidence, and strength, but the Israelites "would not." Will that also be said of us?

"Though I am always in a haste, I am never in a
hurry, because I never undertake more work than I
can go through with perfect calmness of spirit."

JOHN WESLEY

LOVE: THE MARK OF THE CHRISTIAN

By this shall all men know that ye are my disciples,
if ye have love one to another.

JOHN 13:35

It takes an unselfish person to truly love others. That's best exemplified by God in sacrificing His Son for us and by Jesus, who laid down His innocent life for our sins. Grasping the love of God enables us to love others in turn, thus proving that we're Christ's disciples.

Yes, love banishes selfishness. In loving others, we put their needs before our own. We see others through the eyes of Christ, feeling compassion as we help them through their trials. We tend to their wounds as did the Good Samaritan. We break bread with them as did the early Christians as recorded in the book of Acts.

Love is our badge. We must wear it with humility even as we lay down our lives for others. It's called being Christlike.

"Jesus Christ has given us a great evidence of his love to us, he bled love at every vein; therefore we are to imitate him, and as befits Christians, to love one another."

THOMAS WATSON

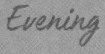

YES, EVEN OUR ENEMIES

Love your enemies, bless them that curse you,
do good to them that hate you, and pray for them
which despitefully use you, and persecute you.

MATTHEW 5:44

Loving one's friends and family is understandable. Even unbelievers do that. But the love of God is a radical love directed even toward His enemies. Now, as Christ's disciples, we may have been surprised to hear that we're to love not just other disciples but our enemies as well. Again, we find God's ways are often contrary to man's flawed thinking.

Have you any enemies you need to love in deed? Remember that love isn't often a feeling, that love, like other aspects of the Christian life, can be embraced by faith. Yes, we can love by faith, not feeling. But don't be surprised when the feelings eventually emerge from loving by faith.

> *"To learn how to love is to learn how to live. The lesson*
> *is a long one, but it is the great business of life to master*
> *it. The Master not only taught the lesson in words but*
> *also set it down for us in a life, His own life. To follow*
> *Christ is to practice this great lesson, learning more of*
> *it day by day, until school is out and we go home!"*

J.R. MILLER

OUR FLEETING EMOTIONS

A wrathful man stirreth up strife:
but he that is slow to anger appeaseth strife.

PROVERBS 15:18

God created us with emotions. Emotions are thus good. But like many things in God's creation, emotions can be abused. Negative emotions like uncontrolled anger, fear, and jealousy can have an effect on our spiritual life—and also hurt those we love.

In fact, even some positive emotions, such as levity, desire, and empathy, can lead to an unbalanced life. With this in mind, we must ask a few questions. First, is this emotion in keeping with a Christlike life? Second, am I able to control my emotions, or do they control me? Do my emotions affect other people? And finally, does this present emotion lead me to a positive or negative action?

"It is Christ who is to be exalted, not our feelings. We
will know Him by obedience, not by emotions. Our
love will be shown by obedience, not by how good
we feel about God at a given moment."

ELISABETH ELLIOT

CONTROL OUR MOODS

He that hath no rule over his own spirit
is like a city that is broken down, and without walls.

PROVERBS 25:28

The person driven by their emotions will likely be unstable in several areas of life, including their spirituality. For instance, if a person suffers from depression that's caused by mood changes, it can lead to doubting God, to moving even further from a healthy emotional state. And under emotional stress, we may question realities that we once accepted as valid. Thus, staying on track emotionally is conducive to continued Christian growth.

Are there some emotions you need help managing? If you can do so with God's help, make it a priority. If you need professional help, seek it. There's no shame in getting help from a qualified Christian counselor.

"Faith is the art of holding on to things your reason has
once accepted in spite of your changing moods."

C.S. LEWIS

GIVE GOD ROOM

With God nothing shall be impossible.
LUKE 1:37

With us, many things are impossible…and so we pray to the One for whom all things are possible. Having prayed, we must then give God room to answer in *His* way, not ours.

Eternity will reveal why it had to be so and will also comfort us with the knowledge that God heard every prayer we uttered. There is no request that our Lord considers too small to answer. And there is no request that He considers too big to answer.

Those of us who face severe trials have a special challenge: We must guard against lacking trust that God will answer, and we must resist the temptation to give up praying too soon when we see no change. In many cases, *persistent* prayer is what gives God room to act.

Whatever your need today, large or small…*trust and persist*.

"Prayers are deathless. They outlive the lives of those who uttered them."
E.M. BOUNDS

SOME TASKS ARE
JUST TOO BIG FOR US

Ah Lord GOD! behold, thou hast made the heaven
and the earth by thy great power and stretched out arm,
and there is nothing too hard for thee.

JEREMIAH 32:17

If we ever wonder why God allows certain situations to reach the crisis stage, we might consider that such occasions virtually force us from depending on our efforts and require us to rely totally on God to intervene.

Would we really believe in prayer—could we really trust in God—if we were never put in the position of casting our need entirely on Him? Like a muscle exercised, faith exercised is strengthened. When God sends difficult situations, even if we are the apparent cause, we can look at it as our Lord inviting Himself into our situation. Will we now trust Him in even *this* impossible predicament?

Every new crisis sets the stage for God to work. The sooner we recognize the impossibility of our prayer, the sooner God can step in.

"Difficulties provide a platform on which
the Lord can display His power."
HUDSON TAYLOR

DELIGHTING IN GOD'S LAW

I have remembered thy name, O LORD,
in the night, and have kept thy law.
PSALM 119:55

God's law reveals God's plan for man. But man couldn't keep God's law, so Christ fulfilled the law on our behalf. Does that mean we no longer have a law in which we're to delight?

Not at all.

It's *still* God's plan that we avoid sin and love His law—even as Paul and James both remind us that we're now under a new law, one that Paul calls the "law of the Spirit of life in Christ Jesus" (Romans 8:2) and James calls the "law of liberty" (James 1:25; 2:12). Delighting in God and His law is still the Lord's will for us, centuries after the psalmist advocated it. Unlike the law we could not keep, we are now delighting in a new law that keeps us.

"O, Holy Spirit, work more powerfully
and thoroughly in us, that we may hate sin,
and delight in God's holy law more and more!"
JAMES SMITH

DELIGHTING IN GOD

Delight thyself also in the LORD:
and he shall give thee the desires of thine heart.

PSALM 37:4

Just as we're to delight ourselves in God's law, so are we also to delight in God Himself. This time, our delight comes with the promise of our heart's desire.

The nearer we draw to God with delight, the more we find that our desires are His desires and that He wills those desires into being on our behalf.

There is a kind of irony in that delighting in God brings not only the blessing of enjoying God, but also the extra blessing of our heart's desire.

Such a promise should prompt us to carefully consider what our heart truly yearns and longs for…for that is what we shall have.

So great is this promise that no one has ever regretted delighting in the Lord.

> *"The more we enjoy of God,*
> *the more we are ravished with delight."*
> THOMAS WATSON

A SERVANT'S LIFE

Let this mind be in you, which was also in Christ Jesus:
who, being in the form of God, thought it not robbery to be
equal with God: but made himself of no reputation,
and took upon him the form of a servant,
and was made in the likeness of men.

PHILIPPIANS 2:5-7

It boggles the mind to think of Jesus Christ, the Lord of lords, innocent as He was, coming to earth to die for the sins of the ungodly. In so doing, Jesus became a servant. He made Himself of no reputation and took on our human form for all of us. How then should we respond? Certainly with a life of thanksgiving, but also as servants, just as He was a servant. What rights does a servant have with his or her master? *None.* In obeying the call to be God's servants, we surrender all our rights. We expect nothing but are astonished at what our Master has promised us. Though we have no rights, we have golden promises.

Serve on, then. Be God's joyful servant. We serve a wonderful Master!

"The servant is nothing,
but God is everything."

HARRY IRONSIDE

THE WAY TO BE EXALTED

He that is greatest among you shall be your servant.
And whosoever shall exalt himself shall be abased;
and he that shall humble himself shall be exalted.

MATTHEW 23:11-12

Humility is in our DNA as God's children. But we don't always live according to our DNA. We need experiences and models to know how to live as we should. Thankfully, God provides both. He often places us in situations where experience becomes our teacher. And as for models of humility, we need look no further than to Christ Himself.

Jesus modeled true humility for us in His role as a servant. There was no pride of self to be found in Christ, and neither should there be in us.

If we choose to exalt ourselves, we will be humbled (and ashamed). But if we humble ourselves, we will be exalted. We have opportunities every day to be humble (not merely *act* humble). And remember, humility comes from contrasting who we would be without Christ versus who we are because of Christ.

> *"It is a contradiction to be a true*
> *Christian and not humble."*
>
> RICHARD BAXTER

THE BEAUTY OF
THE LORD UPON US

Let the beauty of the LORD our God be upon us.
PSALM 90:17

We don't often think of ourselves as beautiful, though that's how God sees us. We are a part of His creation—the one that in Genesis He pronounced as "very good." Yes, sin has taken its toll, and we, like creation, live under the curse of the fall. Yet in spite of the surrounding sin that defiles us, the psalmist has the audacity to plea for the beauty of the Lord our God to be upon us. That's a request God will grant to each of us—an acknowledgment of the beauty we still have within us.

Today, think of yourself with the beauty of the Lord upon you. Look not in your own mirror, but see yourself in the mirror God holds before you.

"Humanity was made to be beautiful. God's ideal for man was spotless loveliness; man was made at first, in God's image. But sin has left its foul trail everywhere! We see something of its debasement wherever we go. What ruins sin has wrought! All of Christ's work of grace, is towards the restoration of the beauty of the Lord in His people."
J.R. MILLER

ESTABLISH THE
WORK OF OUR HANDS

Establish thou the work of our hands upon us;
yea, the work of our hands establish thou it.
PSALM 90:17

At its heart, the Christian life is a satisfied life. God has chosen our lot, given us work to do, and filled us with Himself. Our work here is sustained by prayer and by trusting God that He will establish the work of our hands, whatever endeavor that might be. Indeed, it's no small thing to consider that God has carefully arranged a productive and joyful life for us, despite the trials we face. His will trumps any sense of adversity that befalls us, for we know God wastes nothing in conforming us to the image of Christ.

Tonight, consider afresh the work of your hands. Thank God for the fruit of that work. Be it small or large, we each have a part to play in God's plan.

"Oh, satisfy us early with Your mercy, that we may rejoice and
be glad all our days. Let the beauty of the Lord our God be
upon us, and establish the work of our hands upon us."
J.R. MILLER

TRIALS AND TRIBULATIONS ARE A PART OF LIFE

These things I have spoken unto you, that in me ye
might have peace. In the world ye shall have tribulation:
but be of good cheer; I have overcome the world.

JOHN 16:33

God's Word is always true. And we surely know Jesus was speaking truth when He said we'd have tribulation in this world.

When we encounter various tribulations, we rarely thank God for them. Truth be told, we want them to be gone. But life without trials would not be a life wherein we would have reasons to lean hard on God in prayer. After all, it's usually during our rough patches that we find ourselves praying in earnest.

Are you suffering from a tribulation now? If not, it's likely you soon will be. Be prepared to accept the peace Christ brings during life's trials. And thank God, even as you pray for Him to bring resolution. The greater the trial, the greater the degree to which God's peace will be provided.

"Many men owe the grandeur of their lives
to their tremendous difficulties."

CHARLES SPURGEON

FOR EVERY TRIAL,
GOD HAS AN ANSWER

*If any of you lack wisdom, let him ask of God,
that giveth to all men liberally, and upbraideth not;
and it shall be given him. But let him ask in faith,
nothing wavering. For he that wavereth is like a
wave of the sea driven with the wind and tossed.*

JAMES 1:5-6

Every trial has the right resolution—the God-ordered resolution. The hard part for us is realizing what the resolution is and waiting for it to make itself known.

We may be surprised at a new trial, but God isn't. And He knows the ultimate right resolution. Our part is to pray that resolution into being as we watch the trial unfold. Trials have odd ways of going one way, then zigzagging in another direction. But God is aware of those surprises well before we are.

As you pray, ask God for His solution, then watch (with thankfulness) and see how He resolves it.

*"As God is exalted to the right place in our lives,
a thousand problems are solved all at once."*

A.W. TOZER

SUBMIT TO GOD

Submit yourselves therefore to God.

JAMES 4:7

Submission is hard for us—that is, until we reach the point of desperation and let go of the situation because we've exhausted all known remedies. Though it's often the large trials that bring us to our knees, God wants our submission to Him in *all* aspects of our life.

Sometimes God allows certain stresses for the exact purpose of causing us to submit to Him, letting go of our own hold, setting aside all our human resources to make way for His power to take over.

Submission, like all else in the Christian life, is by faith. Today, feelings aside, cast your lot with God. Submit your life in its entirety to your heavenly Father.

"The cause of the weakness of your Christian life is that you want to work it out partly, and to let God help you. And that cannot be. You must come to be utterly helpless, to let God work, and God will work gloriously."

ANDREW MURRAY

RESIST THE DEVIL

Resist the devil, and he will flee from you.

JAMES 4:7

Submission to God opens the pathway to great victory in our Christian life. But there's more. We all have a deadly enemy, one whose strategies are designed to destroy our faith and ultimately our souls. After submitting to God, we must do the converse to the devil: We must resist him. When we do so, he will flee. He may suggest a thought to you, but you have the power to reject the suggestion. At such times, God may also be suggesting a far better thought. Accept His thoughts immediately. And remember: Developing the habit of rejecting evil thoughts and replacing them with godly thoughts will save us much heartache. Plus, there is great joy in seeing our enemy on the run. So, no matter Satan's present strategy—whether circumstantial, relational, physical, financial, or mental—send your enemy on his way by submitting to God and resisting the devil's attempts to bring you down.

> *"In resisting there is strength, comfort, victory, and peace. Temptation yielded to is sin. Temptation resisted and overcome, is victory. It is God's command that we should resist. It is God's promise that we shall overcome."*
>
> FRANCIS BOURDILLON

OUR FAITHFUL GOD

If we believe not, yet he abideth faithful:
he cannot deny himself.

2 TIMOTHY 2:13

Throughout life we encounter people who let us down. At best, they simply couldn't comply with their promises. At worst, they lied to us. And we're not always so innocent ourselves. Sometimes we were the guilty party—we were unfaithful.

It's so reassuring to fathom the depths of God, the only being with whom there is never duplicity, unrighteousness, or broken promises. God is simply always faithful. His Word can be trusted, His character unassailable, His promises secure. In all this, He never changes. Even when we "believe not," God remains faithful. That's just His nature.

May God help us to be unfailingly faithful, just like our Father.

"Far above all finite comprehension, is the unchanging faithfulness
of God. Everything about God is great, vast, incomparable. He
never forgets, never fails, never falters, never forfeits His word."

A.W. PINK

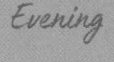

DECLARING GOD'S FAITHFULNESS

I have declared thy faithfulness and thy salvation:
I have not concealed thy lovingkindness and
thy truth from the great congregation.

PSALM 40:10

It can be hard or at least awkward telling others about Christ, but one way is to be open to declaring His faithfulness. Sometimes, perhaps out of fear, we neglect to mention the faithfulness of God when a hard situation has been resolved.

Even if we simply declare His constancy to ourselves, that's a step forward. The truth is that God is faithful in thousands of ways every day…we just don't always notice.

As you unwind from today's events, can you recall ways (large or small) that reflect God's faithfulness? Can you recall your own fidelity today?

"Let the last sounds of evening bear testimony to His faithfulness.
Thus let each day declare that loving and faithful is the Lord."

HENRY LAW

PREACHING TO OURSELVES

*Why art thou cast down, O my soul? and why art thou
disquieted in me? hope thou in God: for I shall yet
praise him for the help of his countenance.*

PSALM 42:5

There are several places in the Psalms where the writer instructs his soul to "yet praise him." So, too, can we engage in self-talk that sets our day aright even as it begins. Here, the psalmist questioned why his soul was cast down, and then he offered the cure: hoping in God and praising Him.

Truthfully, every one of our days should begin with praise and a fresh admonition to our souls to hope in God. Thus we set the tone for the day. Talk to your soul this morning. Instruct yourself to praise God for a fresh day.

*"I saw more clearly than ever, that the first great and primary
business to which I ought to attend every day was, to have
my soul happy in the Lord. The first thing to be concerned
about was not, how much I might serve the Lord, how I
might glorify the Lord; but how I might get my soul into a
happy state, and how my inner man may be nourished."*

GEORGE MUELLER

MY JOYFUL SOUL

I will greatly rejoice in the LORD, my soul shall be joyful
in my God; for he hath clothed me with the garments of
salvation, he hath covered me with the robe of righteousness,
as a bridegroom decketh himself with ornaments,
and as a bride adorneth herself with her jewels.

ISAIAH 61:10

Isaiah made sure his soul was joyful in God—and he had good reason for such joy. He was clothed by God with the garments of salvation and covered with the robe of righteousness. But then so are we. We too have cause to rejoice greatly in the Lord. We can do so at the start of each day, but also as each day ends. No matter what today has held, even if you don't feel like it, insist that your soul be joyful in the Lord your God. Be steadfast in this. Start with words of praise, and your soul will soon follow.

"There is nothing dreary and doubtful about [life]. It
is meant to be continually joyful.... We are called to a
settled happiness in the Lord whose joy is our strength."

AMY CARMICHAEL

GODLY STEADFASTNESS

Be ye stedfast, unmoveable, always abounding in
the work of the Lord, forasmuch as ye know that
your labor is not in vain in the Lord.

1 CORINTHIANS 15:58

The word for today is *steadfast*. Paul encouraged the Corinthian believers to be steadfast and, in so doing, admonishes us also. Our steadfastness is to be found in our abounding work of the Lord, for we know our labor is not in vain.

Consider that our work *without* the Lord *is* in vain—and we will likely find ourselves not steadfast but movable, varying from one thing to the next.

Today each of us can resolve to be unmovable and focused on our work for the Lord. Even if our work is of a secular nature, we are called to be faithful and productive. Our jobs are of God's choosing and thus part of the work to which He has called us, and they can be done for His glory.

"The more high and improved a man's graces are the more
that man will do for God; and the more any man does
for God, the more at last shall he receive from God."

THOMAS BROOKS

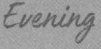

I SHALL NOT BE MOVED

He only is my rock and my salvation:
he is my defense; I shall not be moved.

PSALM 62:6

In today's world there are many things that try to move us from our steadfast trust in the Lord. If not rejected, these whispers to compromise will become louder in the future. The time to root ourselves unmovably in the Lord is well before the storms come.

We must all be ready to stand on the rock as our faith is ridiculed, scoffed at, and belittled. We must also encourage others to stand on the rock with us, confident in the knowledge that it can hold all who will join us.

"My Rock shall stand fast forever, when the foundations of
the earth are moved, and the pillars of heaven tremble!
There shall I be safe, when the hail shall sweep away
the refuges of lies; yes, when God shall rain on sinners—
snares, fire, and brimstone, in the furious storm of
wrath, I shall sing in safety, being an inhabitant of the
Rock of ages, from which I never shall be moved!"

JAMES MEIKLE

SEALED!

*In whom ye also trusted, after that ye heard the word
of truth, the gospel of your salvation: in whom also after that
ye believed, ye were sealed with that holy Spirit of promise.*

EPHESIANS 1:13

When God seals something, it *stays* sealed. All of us who have trusted the word of truth and believed the gospel are sealed, not with an earthly seal but with the seal of the Holy Spirit of promise. Both God's seal and His promise are as secure as His character. We have no need to fear being cast aside by God. The fact is, our seal was ratified by the blood of the Son. There is full security in knowing that the Lord has sealed us as His own.

*"We have a divine, authoritative rule of life, a code of directions
of the amplest, fullest, minutest character, intended and
sufficient to regulate and control every thought, word, and
action of our lives; and all flowing from the eternal wisdom
and will of the Father, sealed and ratified by the blood of
the Son, and inspired and revealed by the Holy Spirit."*

J.C. PHILPOT

THE EARNEST
OF THE SPIRIT

He which stablisheth us with you in Christ,
and hath anointed us, is God; who hath also sealed us,
and given the earnest of the Spirit in our hearts.

2 CORINTHIANS 1:21-22

The seal of God has been described as a down payment (or earnest money) for that which is to come. Down payments are only given when the certainty of the purchase has been decided. God has made the irreversible decision that He wants us. Though the price has been paid by Christ on the cross, the Holy Spirit has been given us as a further guarantee of God's choosing us. Having thus decided, God cannot and will not refuse us. He never has buyer's remorse.

"If God have sealed, he will not refuse you;
if he have given his earnest, he will not shut
you out; God's earnest is not given in jest."

JOHN FLAVEL

EVERY DAY A BLESSING

Cause me to hear thy lovingkindness in the morning;
for in thee do I trust: cause me to know the way wherein
I should walk; for I lift up my soul unto thee.

PSALM 143:8

What a way to begin the day—hearing the loving-kindness of the Lord in the early hours, lifting up our souls to God, trusting Him for a day whose events are yet to unfold, believing He will cause us to know the way wherein we should walk.

Though we awake never knowing for sure what the day holds, we do know that as we slept, God fashioned the day ahead according to His will and to our benefit. How, then, can we not begin our day with prayer and praise?

"Praise has a wonderful lifting power! We need not be
anxious about the outcome of things, if we will but take
the attitude of deliverance and begin to praise."

LETTIE COWMAN

IN THE NIGHT SEASONS

I will bless the Lord, who hath given me counsel:
my reins also instruct me in the night seasons.

PSALM 16:7

We may have good counselors surrounding us, but in the Lord we have the best of all counselors—one who trumps all others. Not only is His counsel available during the day, but He also instructs us in the night seasons. True, His fees are fairly exorbitant in that He requires all of us if we would have all of Him. But the deal is still in our favor—and for His good counsel, we bless the Lord!

"God's goodness is near us. It is not a goodness far away, but God
follows us with His goodness in whatever situation we are. He
attaches Himself to us, He has made Himself close, that He
might be near us in goodness. He is a father, and everywhere to
maintain us. He is a husband, and everywhere to help. He is a
friend, and everywhere to comfort and counsel. His love is a near
love. He has taken upon Himself the closest kinds of relationships,
so that we may never lack God and the evidences of His love."

RICHARD SIBBES

OUR SPIRITUAL RESOURCES

My God shall supply all your need
according to his riches in glory by Christ Jesus.
PHILIPPIANS 4:19

Every Christian has all the necessary resources to meet life's challenges. No difficulty or problem can befall us in which God can't supply the exact solution. How does He do this? It's all according to His riches in Christ Jesus. And what riches are greater than those to be found in Christ Jesus? It's not possible that we should require riches God cannot give. The catch is that these riches—and every necessary resource—are only available to believers. Though we may avail ourselves of certain natural resources, they pale in comparison to God's supply of heavenly riches. Perhaps today you will need to draw from your heavenly supply. Do so freely and joyfully, confident in the knowledge that God loves to meet our needs by His riches in Christ Jesus.

"All the resources of God are for those who are for Him."
JAMES SMITH

NATURAL RESOURCES

The natural man receiveth not the things of the Spirit of God:
for they are foolishness unto him: neither can he know them,
because they are spiritually discerned.

1 CORINTHIANS 2:14

For many of our problems, natural resources will be of some help. But where natural resources end, spiritual resources stand waiting. The gifts of nature are available to all, but the gifts of the Lord can be accessed only through the Spirit and only by believers in Christ.

If we mention spiritual resources to an unbeliever, we may sound foolish. It takes spiritual discernment to tap into and comprehend spiritual resources. Many believers fail at solving problems because they're either unaware of these resources or simply willing to rely on natural resources alone.

"Natural strength is what we receive from the
hand of God as Creator. Spiritual strength is
what we receive from God in grace."

WATCHMAN NEE

THE INCORRUPTIBLE WORD

Being born again, not of corruptible seed,
but of incorruptible, by the word of God,
which liveth and abideth for ever.

1 PETER 1:23

When we were born again, it was through the incorruptible seed: the Word of God. And so for the rest of our earthly lives we continue to feed on—feast on!—the Word. The Bible is meat for meals, water for thirst, life in place of death. This is why we must immerse ourselves in the Word often. Going without a meal in the Word causes hunger, and hunger unsatisfied leads to starvation and death. You will have time to plant some of the incorruptible Word in your heart today. Other matters may press you, but if you want life, don't pass up time in the Word.

"Within believers there is a living and incorruptible seed which
lives and abides forever; why should they envy mere flesh, and
the glory of it, which are but as grass, and the flower thereof?"

CHARLES SPURGEON

LIVING THE WORD

*My son, attend to my words; incline thine ear unto my
sayings. Let them not depart from thine eyes; keep them in
the midst of thine heart. For they are life unto those
that find them, and health to all their flesh.*

PROVERBS 4:20-22

When Solomon gave advice to his son, he made sure that
son understood the importance of his advice. It was not to
depart from his eyes; it was to be kept in the midst of his heart. And
why? Because his words were the words of *life*.

So important is God's Word to us, in fact, that we ignore it at our
own peril, for His Word is life itself to believers. If we would have
life, we must have the Word.

Tonight, incline your ear to God's words to you—and be healthy.

*"O, for greater love to the Scriptures—that we may know
them, enjoy them, conform to them, exercise faith in them,
and make them our delight! May we read them daily, pray
over them constantly, meditate on them frequently, and
manifest their holy tendency in life and death. May our
memories be stored with them, our hearts be sanctified
by them, and our lives correspond with them."*

JAMES SMITH

Wisdom for Life

The **KJV Devotional for Men** features exquisitely written Scripture verses, quotes, and short spiritual applications that offer insights on…

Valuing silence—*Be still, and know that I am God* (Psalm 46:10).

Loving one another—*This is my commandment, That ye love one another as I have loved you* (John 15:12).

Seeking and granting forgiveness—*Be ye kind one to another, tenderhearted, forgiving one another, even as God for Christ's sake hath forgiven you* (Ephesians 4:32).

Perfect for gift-giving or personal study.
Available wherever books are sold,

INSIGHTS FOR DAILY LIVING

The ***KJV Devotional for Women*** enlightens and inspires
with beautiful Scripture verses, quotes, and short
spiritual applications encouraging women to…

Choose thankfulness—*In every thing give thanks: for this is the
will of God in Christ Jesus concerning you* (1 Thessalonians 5:18).

Offer praise—*Let everything that hath breath praise
the Lord. Praise ye the Lord* (Psalm 150:6).

Find rest in God—*Come unto me, all ye that labor and are
heavy laden, and I will give you rest* (Matthew 11:28).

Ideal for gifting or to enrich your own daily walk with God.
Available wherever books are sold.

MORE GREAT DEVOTIONALS
FROM NICK HARRISON

ONE-MINUTE PRAYERS®
WHEN YOU NEED A MIRACLE

When life looks bleak and you need God to show up in a big way, *One-Minute Prayers® When You Need a Miracle* connects your needs to God's promises as time in prayer stretches your faith and enlarges your view of God.

ONE-MINUTE PRAYERS®
FOR HUSBANDS

Discover biblical encouragement in this collection of prayers and devotions written for busy husbands who need a minute of inspiration.

ONE-MINUTE PRAYERS®
FOR DADS

These brief prayers will help dads connect with God as they thank Him for their kids and ask Him for what they need to be the best fathers they can be.

ONE-MINUTE PRAYERS®
FOR THOSE WITH CANCER

These encouraging writings will lead readers from fear to faith in the face of illness.

To learn more about Harvest House books and
to read sample chapters, visit our website:

www.HarvestHousePublishers.com

HARVEST HOUSE PUBLISHERS
EUGENE, OREGON